# Cruise
## THE UNAUTHORIZED BIOGRAPHY

# Cruise

## THE UNAUTHORIZED BIOGRAPHY

## FRANK SANELLO

TAYLOR PUBLISHING COMPANY
Dallas, Texas

Published by Taylor Publishing Company
                1550 West Mockingbird Lane
                Dallas, Texas 75235

**Library of Congress Cataloging-in-Publication Data**

Sanello, Frank.
        Cruise : the unauthorized biography / Frank Sanello.
            p.        cm.
        ISBN 0-87833-913-2
            1. Cruise, Tom, 1962–    .2. Motion picture actors and actresses—
United States—Biography.   I.  Title.
        PN2287.C685S26    1995
        791.43'028'092—dc20
        [B]                                                                95-24499
                                                                            CIP

Published in the United States of America

10  9  8  7  6  5  4  3  2  1

This book is printed on acid-free recycled paper.

*For my four-legged family in fur coats: Wendy, Marshmallow, Pasta, Gremlin, George, Lucrezia, Cesare, Falstaff, Bunny, Luigi, Thisbe, and Catullus*

# Contents

# ACKNOWLEDGEMENTS

For a lifetime of inspiration and assistance: Dr. Andrew Faulk, Robert V. Buckley, Morgan Gendel, and Professor David Williams.

For their incisive insights: Dr. Kate Wachs, Demi Moore, Dustin Hoffman, Rob Reiner, David Geffen, Anne Rice, Robert Duvall, Barry Levinson, David Ehrenstein, Paul Newman, Rebecca De Mornay, Pat Kingsley, Lisa Goodman, Kevin Pollack, Elizabeth Shue, Bertram Fields, Don Simpson, Jerry Bruckheimer, Father Mel Brady, Francis Coppola, Ron Howard, Ron Kovic, Randy Quaid, Kelly McGillis, Shelley Long, Jack Nicholson, Diane Lane, Mimi Rogers, Martin Scorsese, Steven Spielberg, Tony Scott, Sydney Pollack, Gene Hackman, Robert Towne, Oliver Stone, Kevin Bacon, David Marlow, Steve Ginsberg, and all the overworked and underpaid staff at the Academy of Motion Picture Arts & Sciences Library.

Also: I have included in this book portions of interviews I have conducted with Tom Cruise over the many years I have worked in Hollywood as an entertainment journalist, most notably an in-depth interview I conducted with Mr. Cruise in July 1988 at the Westwood Marquis Hotel in Los Angeles.

# Preface

Tom Cruise lives on a pleasant but not palatial estate in Pacific Palisades, California. This manicured suburb of Los Angeles is not as "old money" as Beverly Hills or as sumptuous as Holmby Hills where "fixer-uppers" start at $3 million, but it is near the Pacific Ocean, and the air is noticeably cleaner than in many pricier enclaves on the Westside's Platinum Triangle. Stallone lives there. So does Arnold. The place seems to attract box-office royalty.

Cruise bought the house for $4.7 million in August 1990, four months before his marriage to second wife and frequent co-star Nicole Kidman. It's a colonial-style home with electric gates. Two stories encompass five bedrooms, five and a half baths, four fireplaces, and a roomy 6,200 square feet. After closing escrow, the couple spent millions more fixing the place up.

The price tag, which for mere mortals would be prohibitive, actually represents a certain frugality on Cruise's part, since $4.7 million is about a third of his price per film. And since he makes an average of two films a year, the mortgage is only one sixth of his annual income. This is not a man who lives beyond his means—by any means.

"Tom is *nouveau riche*," says an associate, "but he doesn't act like your typical *nouveau riche* movie star. He could buy and sell most of the people in Hollywood, but he doesn't flaunt his wealth. By the way he dresses and acts, if you didn't know he was Tom Cruise, you'd think he was just another regular schmo, albeit quite a very attractive schmo."

Cruise's relative parsimony is only one of the aftershocks of his childhood, which was frugal by necessity, not choice. Even more relevant to his past is the layout of the estate. The house is fronted by a long, tree-lined driveway, perfectly designed to keep enquiring minds and photographers at arm's (and zoom lens's) length. This self-imposed isolation also echoes his childhood—where the isolation was not of his choosing.

"He's not Howard Hughes by any means," another source who knows him says. "But he's not a social gadabout. He doesn't hang out 'til closing time at trendy clubs. He's only thirty-two, but his social life is practically nonexistent. If he didn't have to report to movie sets, he'd be a virtual hermit."

As Cruise looks out of the window of his "modest" mansion at a breathtaking view of the Pacific Ocean, one wonders if the superstar contrasts his present digs with his impoverished childhood. Does he reflect on the bad old days when the fatherless family went on food stamps? Does he think about that one Christmas, which has been enshrined in Cruise lore, when his mother didn't have cash for presents so Tom and his three sisters wrote each other poems instead?

On those rare occasions when he makes a public appearance and exchanges his torn jeans and white T-shirt for an Armani suit and Gucci shoes, does he remember the humiliation of having to wear cousins' hand-me-downs that were not only unfashionable but didn't even fit? Or going to the senior prom in a baggy suit two sizes too large so he would be able to wear it for years to come?

As he's surrounded by well-paid yes-men and groveling studio executives who would trade their first-born children for a Cruise project on their release schedules, does Tom remember having no friends in high school because his family was always moving from city to city every few years?

As he personally manages his multimillion-dollar investment portfolio without the help of a business manager—unheard of among Hollywood's gilded class—does he remember feeling stupid because his undiagnosed dyslexia dumped him in a remedial class for slow learners?

Does he think about his ex-wife's vicious comments questioning his virility in an interview with *Playboy*? Does his messy divorce remind him of his parents' divorce and the disastrous effects it had on the family's living standards?

And as he endears himself to father-figure co-stars like Dustin Hoffman and Paul Newman, does he remember his own disengaged dad, who never saw a single one of his son's films before his death a decade ago?

"Tom is still looking for Daddy," says an associate who's known him for years. "You can see it in the way he attaches himself to the older stars on the set. Most guys his age, especially with his super success, tend to act cocky. You know, the James Dean/Marlon Brando rebel-without-a-cause kind of jerk. Tom is an old soul in a young body. Maybe he relates to fifty-something stars like Gene Hackman and Robert Duvall so well because deep down inside Tom is in his fifties as well. Tom is no Brat Packer. If you had to compare him to any movie star, he's more like Gary Cooper with a bit of Tony Curtis's sense of fun thrown in."

The memories he mulls over in his lonely mansion aren't all bad. As he pals around with his self-described "best friend," the second Mrs. Cruise, Nicole Kidman, does he realize his love of women comes from a childhood filled with positive female role models like his devoted mom and three sisters, who worshipped the only man in the house?

We may never know the answers to all these questions, for Tom Cruise in recent years has become a male Garbo, inaccessible to the press and public. Never the most gregarious of public figures, Cruise has become increasingly more isolated. Some blame his new-found religion, the cult-like Church of Scientology. Others say his press-hating publicists have kept him out of the limelight.

And yet this is the same man who, when he does agree to a rare interview to promote his umpteenth film, is unfailingly polite, calling his interviewer "Ma'am" or "Sir." No Sean Penn antics. None of Demi Moore's infamous unpunctuality at press conferences.

"He treats you with an almost Oriental politeness," says someone who's worked with him before. "He's so deferential, it's hard to believe this is one of the richest and most powerful figures in the movie business."

Despite an increasingly cold and aloof public image, this is the same man who ripped off his tuxedo jacket at a post-Oscar party at Spago to cover his shivering, bare-shouldered wife. This is also the man who helped a photographer to his feet after the man fell during a photo-op at a movie premiere—Cruise's fellow celebrities laughed and stepped over the prone paparazzo.

Colleagues ranging from temperamental superstars like Dustin Hoffman to tyrannical directors like Oliver Stone all praise the deferential young man for being the most un-star-like of stars. Never a prima donna, always punctual, he is the antithesis of the Movie Star From Hell.

A Hollywood insider notes, "Tom is the most egoless of superstars. Everyone who works with him falls just a little bit in love with him. That's easy to do because he is just a lovable kind of guy. He's not snooty. He's extremely cooperative and giving on the set. Every director who's ever worked with him would love to repeat the experience, and that's not because his films are so commercially successful. Directors just like working with a star who can take direction without trying to one-up the guy in charge, namely the director."

We can only hope to answer our questions by means of some serious sleuthing, for Tom Cruise is unlikely ever to provide the answers himself.

It is possible, however, to understand Tom Cruise, current king of the box-office hill, by examining the troubled, lonely, fatherless childhood and adolescence of Thomas Cruise Mapother IV. His is an archetypal story of rags (literally) to riches, an all-American success story of a poor boy who became a multimillionaire, now on his way to becoming a billionaire. Of a lonely adolescent who married not one but two of the most beautiful women in Hollywood.

"Tom Cruise is living the American dream. No, that's not right," says another Hollywood observer who knows the actor. "Tom is living the American dream that most of us can only dream about. It's an idealized version of that dream."

If Horatio Alger had lived to see Hollywood today, he could have used Tom Cruise's life as a template for his rags-to-riches tales. Instead, we will stand in for Mr. Alger and show how Cruise's troubled formative years actually strengthened him and provided the tools to achieve the pinnacle of both personal and commercial success.

Sadly, the price he has paid, that he is still paying, for success is an increasing isolation that ironically recreates the loneliness of his deprived youth. Cruise may again be lonely, but at least his loneliness is lived out in the trappings of luxury and adulation—from afar.

# Cruise
## THE UNAUTHORIZED BIOGRAPHY

# ONE

# The Vagabond Prince

H is name alone speaks volumes that he will probably never speak himself. The world's most successful star is not the famous Thomas Cruise Mapother IV. He's simply Tom Cruise. Someone with a psychoanalytic bent might hypothesize that the actor consciously cut his father's name out of his life. No other explanation comes to mind, since "Mapother" is a much more resonant "movie star" name than "Cruise."

Thomas Cruise Mapother IV (the name is still on his drivers' license) was born the day *before* the Fourth of July, 1962, in Syracuse, New York. The Mapothers were solid middle class. Dad, a graduate of the University of Louisville, was an electrical salesman and would-be inventor. His job necessitated uprooting the family every few years and relocating to a new city.

Early on, Tom demonstrated a precocious lust for adventure. At the age of two, he would wander outside the house. At four, he would travel further, to a pond near his home, to commune with nature. His frantic mother would call the police to retrieve the errant toddler.

Later his wander-lust became involuntary and painful. Following his father's peripatetic job requirements, young Tom attended eight elementary schools and three high schools during

1

a lonely youth that was both figuratively and literally dislocated.

Cruise's mother, Mary Lee, had acting aspirations of her own, which she abandoned to raise her son and three daughters. Tom was the second youngest. Mary Lee was also deeply religious, and her philosophical take on life's hardships kept the family's spirits up, even during times of financial distress, which were to be many and severe.

Perhaps it's his unfailing optimism, or maybe it's just plain old-fashioned denial, but today Cruise claims the constant moving was in some cosmic way good training for his future career. "Some people would think [relocating] would be a horrifying experience. I enjoyed it. Traveling into different environments doesn't threaten me. It was like picking up a part, playing a role along the way. If we went South, I'd pick up a little Southern accent because having a Canadian accent wasn't cool," he once said.

This chameleon-like ability to blend in wherever he went was invaluable training for an actor, who during his career must assume a different identity for every role. The constant moving would turn out to be a boon for his career years later, but it was hell for a young boy desperate to fit in, who never quite made the transition to total acceptance by his peers.

The dislocation, always being the new boy at school, was exacerbated by poverty.

His parents divorced when he was eleven, and his father refused to pay child support for Tom or his three sisters. To feed four children, his mother was forced to work three jobs, and yet the family still found itself slipping inexorably into the lower middle class. A painful memory from childhood, Cruise once recalled, was the sight of his mother weeping because she couldn't give her children the material things other parents could.

"Tom was acutely aware of his family's poverty," says another associate, who requested anonymity. "He grew up surrounded by kids who always had more money than he. Strangely, when he finally got a fortune of his own, he didn't turn into a shopaholic or go on spending sprees. There's still a little bit of the poor boy from Syracuse in the superstar. He's not the kind of guy to flaunt his wealth. Away from his mansion and his Porsche, he looks and acts like anybody else. No gaudy or expensive gold jewelry. In fact, the only jewelry he wears is a wedding ring."

The family was forced to make other economies which added to his sense of dislocation. From time to time, to save money on food, Tom would live with his aunt. And to take more monetary pressure off mom, he mowed lawns and delivered newspapers at four in the morning in driving rains.

But what the fatherless Mapother clan couldn't afford in material things, they more than made up for with spiritual values and plain old-fashioned ingenuity. Money was so tight the first Christmas after his parents' divorce that the cash-strapped Mapothers were forced to give each other "gifts" of poems. For the less poetic family members, making one another's beds was also popular—and dirt cheap! This was also literally the "rags" period of Tom's life, as he found himself wearing ill-fitting and unfashionable hand-me-downs from cousins.

Like his contemporaries, Tom had an obsession with dressing right. Unfortunately, the family's nonexistent clothes budget and frequent moves meant Tom was rarely dressed in the height of fashion or anywhere near it. "I worried a lot about my clothes not being cool," he has said. "We didn't have much money, and just when I'd save enough money to buy the Keds everyone was wearing, we'd move to a town where everyone else was wearing Nikes."

Eventually, the self-reliant young man came to set his own fashion style. And typically precocious at this as with everything else, he achieved this sense of ego stability at an age when most other teenagers are just confronting how rotten and insecure they feel about their looks, their clothes, their complexions, *ad nauseam*. "At fourteen," he would later declare, "I finally learned to be myself."

The next year, Tom was already putting into practice the lessons he had learned about being himself. For the sophomore prom, he shelled out a then whopping $100 for a suit, but anticipating his future fiscal good sense, he bought the outfit two sizes too large so he could wear it long after prom night. The downside, of course, was that he went to the gala event looking like a dork in an ill-fitting suit. "Every time Tom buys a $3,000 Armani suit, I bet he thinks back to the sophomore prom when he paid considerably less for a rag that didn't even fit him. That must make the Armani suit feel all that much better," says an acquaintance.

Today, Cruise refuses to think of his childhood as Dickensian. He has said, "Even the troubled moments of my childhood were quite exciting. I look back on it, and our family was really close. The rough times really brought us together. There was no money, but I know people who had it one hundred times worse than we did. I just looked at it as an adventure."

His mother must have considered it more nightmarish than adventurous. To support four children she worked three jobs simultaneously and moonlighted at trade conventions where she sold electrical appliances. Mom would come home so exhausted, her son tried to cheer her up by massaging her feet every night for six weeks one spring! When she came home the Monday after Easter, and propped her feet up on an ottoman, waiting for her nightly massage, Tom finally said, "Mom, Lent is over."

"Tom adored his mother. He still does. He goes out of his way to treat her like a queen. He remembers how she was always there for him—when she wasn't working three jobs. And now he's there for her. He is a devoted son. But he's also his mother's pal in a weird sort of way. He took her to the Academy Awards one year and went sky diving with her on another occasion. How many guys do you know who are self-confident enough to show up at a major event like the Oscars with their mother in tow?" asks an incredulous associate.

The nadir of the family fortunes came when his mother reluctantly applied for food stamps to feed her brood. But she couldn't go through with the humiliation of using the stamps at the market where she had always shopped. Tom recalled, "One time my mother went to apply for food stamps. She saw all these people, and she said, 'I don't care what it takes. I am *not* coming here again.' My father didn't pay any child support. Once my mother divorced my father, it was just four women and myself."

Years later, when an interviewer kept pestering Cruise to lighten up and give him some amusing quotes, the actor explained why he was such an old soul at the ripe old age of twenty-seven. "You've asked me a couple of times where the seriousness comes from, why it's so different from my image.

"I guess you can't help but grow up fast when your parents get divorced. You see situations where your mother goes to get food stamps and she's making fifty dollars too much to get them and she's got four kids to support. You know, a mother with four kids living off meat pies three times a week."

A colleague comments, "To this day, this zillionaire still feels compelled to clean his plate. He never leaves anything to be thrown out, even though he's rich enough to buy a chain of grocery stores."

Tom was a middle child, the only man in the house. It's a psychological truism that middle children tend to be over-achievers to compensate for the fact that parents tend to "baby" the baby of the family and delegate adult responsibilities to the oldest, leaving the kid in the middle feeling underappreciated.

"Tom wants to be loved," says an associate. "He practically begs you to like him. And he succeeds by being the best friend you could ever have. Everybody who's ever worked with him has felt his friendship. It's like a warm blanket that envelops you with his care and concern. His personality is so sunny, he could cure someone with clinical depression just by osmosis."

It's fortunate for Cruise that he was close to his mother, not his father. He seems to have absorbed all his mother's positive traits, including workaholism and a sincere concern for other people.

Dr. Kate Wachs, a clinical psychologist and magazine columnist, believes that you model yourself after the parent you love. Cruise clearly adores his mother. He lavishes gifts on her and his sisters. He even took Mom to the Oscars one year. Dr. Wachs says, "It's the Scarlett O'Hara syndrome. 'As God is my witness I'll never go hungry again.' Tom may be afraid of being poor. But he saw his mother working hard, and the lesson sank in because he was close to his mother. Somebody who came from a poor background and saw at least one parent working hard, learns that you have to work hard in life if you want to get places. If he had been close to his father and saw him detaching himself from the family, he might have grown up thinking you shouldn't show emotions or affection toward your kids."

For whatever psychological or sociological reasons, Tom turned overachieving into an obsession.

During his first year of high school, Tom lived in Louisville, Kentucky, his mother's hometown, where they had moved after the divorce. The Louisville public schools didn't impress Tom or his mother, but a family that couldn't afford Christmas presents certainly couldn't afford the $4,000-a-year tuition for a private school. So he enrolled in St. Francis Seminary's high school in Cincinnati, where the education was superior and—even better—tuition was free! In return for an excellent, free education, the future Father Cruise would have to give up girls permanently!

After a year of pondering lifelong celibacy, Cruise apparently decided an inferior education at a public school was preferable to lifelong abstinence from the opposite sex. Years later, a reporter asked Cruise how close he had come to becoming Father Thomas Mapother. "Not too close," he said. "I was there for one school session. I remember we used to sneak out of the school on weekends and go to this girl's house in town, sit around, talk, and play spin the bottle. I just realized I loved women too much to give that up," Cruise said.

"Can you imagine Tom as Father Mapother?" asks an acquaintance with a laugh. "He's just too ambitious and full of energy for a life of contemplation and no nooky."

The lower-middle-class youth gave up a lot when he left the seminary. The grounds of St. Francis looked more like a country club than an institution whose members had taken life-long vows of chastity, obedience, and *poverty*. (Cruise had already tasted enough of poverty to know he would make a lousy priest.)

The seminary contained many sports amenities that were perfect for the sports-crazy young Cruise: four playing fields for baseball alone, tennis courts, a handball court, a swimming pool, and an artificial lake. While Franciscan priests may take a vow of poverty, they don't live it, as the seminary showed.

Father Mel Brady taught at St. Francis in the 1950s, twenty years before Cruise briefly contemplated a life of contemplation and no girls. "It was a very nice campus, a big campus for such a small school," the aged Father Mel recalls. "There were lots of trees and even a small wood. Actually, it was more like a little forest. It wasn't cultivated. It was just a natural wood," Father Mel says nostalgically.

After his impoverished home life, St. Francis must have seemed luxurious—except there were no female members other than the tyrannical nuns who worked in the laundry and kitchen. Franciscan priests and brothers served on the faculty.

It was life in a gilded, asexual cage. But at least his budding adolescent urgings gave him something to tell the priest during confession, a weekly ritual which was mandatory at the seminary. Tom remembers making up sins for the confessional, such as taking the Lord's name in vain. Other confessed "sins" were real, however, like "having impure thoughts." The uxorious Cruise would later say with a grin, "I never gave those up!"

Dropping out of the seminary was his future female fans' gain, but it was Tom's academic loss. His freshman year at the seminary was the only time he would ever make the honor roll in his academic career because there was nothing to do on campus but study.

He also learned iron self-discipline in the Catholic high school. One of the seminary's strict rules was that students had to walk on every step leading to the classrooms. Late for class one day, Tom raced up the steps, missing several. A tiny nun who worked in the kitchen grabbed him, whipped him around, and put a chokehold on him. Tom recalled the incident years later with an amused horror that wasn't entirely feigned: "Up against the wall, I thought, 'What the hell? Holy Jesus Christ!' She said, 'Don't you ever, *ever* miss another stair again!'"

That kind of attention to detail sank in. A decade later when he became famous, Tom would become infamous and something of a headache for trying to control every aspect of a film's production, from sound recording systems to publicity stills of the star and his wife.

Although he only spent one session at St. Francis, the effects of a Catholic education often stick with the beneficiary—if that's the right term—for life. Jesuits like to boast, "Give me a boy for the first seven years of his life, and he will be mine for life." Ironically, many who attended parochial schools in the fifties and sixties are now either militant atheists or agnostics with no use for the religion in which they were raised and indoctrinated. A more accurate reworking of the Jesuits' boast might be, "Give me a boy for the first seven years of his life, and you'll be sure to create a lapsed Catholic."

What was considered character-building discipline in the 1950s is recognized today for what it often was, child abuse. Not the sexual molestation scandals, which are another story and don't have any relevance to an examination of Cruise's life, but the run-of-the-mill slaps, punches, paddling, and general abuse often poison the recollections of those who attended parochial school. Even well-behaved students, not just discipline problems, remember being pinched, shoved, and pummeled by clergymen in scary black outfits.

But there must have been something good about parochial education or the institutions would have gone out of business long ago. (St. Francis did go out of business, Father Mel explains, because "there just isn't the vocation there anymore. At the most the seminary never had more than 150 students. When it got down to twenty-five it just wasn't economically feasible to keep it open anymore.")

The Church and its educational arm are best at instilling guilt. And guilt, to paraphrase Michael Milken/Michael Douglas's infamous estimation, can be good. It's not psychologically healthy, but guilt can be a powerful motivating force when it's not crippling.

As an adult, one encounters all sorts of unpleasant things in the workplace that have to be put up with to get ahead. Deadlines have to be met. Absenteeism is bad for one's career. Unquestioning obedience to a boss's often idiotic demands can go a long way in one's climb up the career ladder.

A more positive motivation for good job skills and performance would be loving your work, respecting your boss, and in general being happy to be at your desk. Polls show, however, that a scary eighty percent of Americans hate what they do for a living. How do they cope? How do they do a good day's work?

Guilt is an effective motivating factor. Don't show up for work and you lose your job. Miss too many mortgage payments and the wife and kids are out on the street. Smart off to your obnoxious boss and you get canned. Do a mediocre job and after a while you'll be pounding the pavement looking for a new one.

Guilt is unhealthy, but it works. As the world's most effective inducer of guilt, the Catholic Church is nonpareil.

Cruise may have internalized the guilt he picked up during his brief stay at St. Francis, and guilt may make him put in that extra effort to make the sound system on his films better or personally take the punches in a fight scene or go crashing around a race course without a stunt double, all of which he has done on the set for verisimilitude. As one wise philosopher—and lapsed Catholic—put it, "You don't have to be Protestant to enjoy the Protestant work ethic. Catholics have borrowed the Protestant work ethic, seeded it with major guilt, and made it their own."

Unfortunately, the one thing a Catholic education couldn't do for Cruise was help him cope with a major educational problem. Besides the dislocation of moving from Syracuse, New York, to Louisville, then Ottawa, Canada, and finally Glen Ridge, New Jersey, Tom discovered he had bigger educational problems than always being the new kid on the playground. He suffered from the learning disorder dyslexia, which often makes it impossible for its victims to read or perform other common tasks. Tom literally could not distinguish his right hand from his left.

In an interview to promote *Risky Business* in 1984, Cruise revealed that dyslexia was literally a family problem. His three sisters as well as his mother suffered from the disorder. "It's a hundred percent better now, but I could never remember which way the C's and G's went. When you're in remedial reading classes, the kids think you're retarded or something. Unfortunately, a lot of the teachers don't understand either."

When I asked him about coping with such a debilitating handicap, his answer was not particularly profound. And he was careful to keep any pain out of his voice, as though recalling a long forgotten memory that no longer even bothered him.

Cruise had either repressed the painful feelings or he had genuinely overcome the insecurity his handicap had to have caused him as one of the apparently slower kids in class. When you're worth more than the entire faculty of your high school's lifetime income, it goes a long way toward soothing any feelings of inferiority you may have had in school. "I was always in remedial réading class. It was very embarrassing," he said, without sounding the least bit embarrassed. "It was humiliating to be asked to read aloud in class. My palms would start sweating. If my family hadn't moved around so much, I would have been held back in class, and the problem probably would have been diagnosed earlier."

Instead, he was classified as a slow learner rather than a victim of a learning disorder. The erroneous classification put the bright youngster in remedial classes. Worse than the embarrassment of hand-me-down clothes was being labelled "slow." It was a source of shame that he remembered all the way back in preschool. "For me, [dyslexia] began in kindergarten. I was forced to write with my right hand when I wanted to use my left. I began to reverse letters, and reading became so difficult. I was always put in remedial classes, and I felt ashamed, like we were the dummies," Cruise recalled years later. Despite all his success as an adult, it was obvious that his childhood academic experiences still haunted him and exacerbated his insecurities.

The disorder was a private shame, one he didn't share with peers. "I never told anyone I was dyslexic when I went to a different school," he said in 1986 at the peak of his success from *Top Gun.* "I was in the remedial class, and I was going in as a new student, and I didn't want to be put in a position of being called an outsider when I already was an outsider. When you're growing up, kids think you're dumb if you're in special reading courses."

The problem was still plaguing him in 1986, although later he would claim Scientology helped him realize he was never dyslexic. But back then, he was willing to admit, "For me, it's still easier to pick up an image of a character when he's described to me rather than from the printed page." Cruise had ingeniously figured out how to compensate for a disability that can be emotionally and professionally crippling.

Overcompensation helped him overcome his classroom difficulties. A different form of overcompensation would turn him into a dynamo on movie sets and be a key to his enduring success. "I had to have focus if I wanted to graduate because I really had to listen to what the teachers were saying," he recalled.

"Tom practically invented the word 'focus,'" says one observer who's known Cruise for years. "He has this almost scary ability to zoom in on something and figure out what's wrong and how he can fix it. If he ever ran for president, he would probably have universal health care signed into law during the first one hundred days of the Cruise presidency."

Unlike the professionals who misdiagnosed him at school, Tom's mother, who had taken courses in special education, identified the cause of his reading problems and tutored him on her own. This potential tragedy, which can lock some people into a life on the slow track, actually had a saving grace. His disability made him even closer to his mother.

Always the eternal optimist, Cruise helps mitigate the bitter memories of being misclassified a slow learner. His learning disability taught him to compensate in other ways, and the habits he developed way back then helped him years later in smoking out good scripts with a high visual content. And the handicap added to his already prodigious overachiever bent. "I've had to work extra hard at everything I've done," he said in 1989. "With my reading difficulties, I'd never catch up [in school]. But people would excuse me: 'He's the new kid. We'll just help him through this year.'" In fact, Cruise claims his dyslexia was never "officially" diagnosed by any of the public schools he attended during his peripatetic youth.

Relying on the courses she had taken in special education and her own can-do mind-set, Tom's mother taught him how to compensate for his inability to comprehend the written word. She helped turn her son into a visually oriented person, a knack he would carry over to his film career.

"I had to train myself to focus my attention. I became very visual and learned how to create mental images in order to comprehend what I read," he once explained. "My mother said, 'Look, you're dyslexic, so you'll just have to work harder at what others take for granted.'"

This was no burden for the youthful workaholic. "The motivation had to come from me. I was going into my junior year of high school, and I vowed, 'This time I won't be in the remedial class.' I worked very hard to bring my reading up to grade level so I could feel that I fit in." And of course, as with everything else he set his mind to, Tom managed to propel himself out of the remedial reading class and into the mainstream group.

Although it's never been diagnosed as such, his description of classroom difficulties sounds as though he also suffered from another learning disability called attention deficit disorder or ADD, a problem that also plagued Sylvester Stallone and allegedly Michael Fay, the American teen caned in Singapore in spring 1994.

Whether or not he actually suffered from ADD, Tom remembers it vividly as "lacking focus." He would think to himself, "If I could just focus in on and do something. I know I've got energy and creativity to be great." Later he would credit his new-found religion Scientology with teaching him how to focus. Scientology, he added, even showed him that he had never been dyslexic in the first place. Whatever it was, something worked. Because his powers of concentration became so famous on the set of *Days of Thunder*, the film's producer Don Simpson nicknamed him "Laserhead" for his ability to zoom in on the matter at hand. Cruise, the former dyslexic, also tears apart scripts and rewrites them to suit his vision. Numbers are no problem either. Distrustful of others handling his vast fortune, Cruise serves as his own business manager. Explaining his hands-on approach to money management, he said, "I've fired a lot of people because they want you to feel like the dumb actor:

'Oh, you don't have to worry about this!' I'd tell them, 'No, I sign my own checks. I take care of my own business.'"

To this day, Cruise is grateful for the strong family home-life that helped him deal with his dyslexia and other problems, including financial ones. "I was lucky to be able to talk to my family," he has said. "I worry about kids who don't have anyone to reach out to."

Besides the support of his family, Cruise had other strate-gies for compensating for his learning disabilities. One was to throw himself into athletics, an interest that, in a strange way, led him to acting. As with everything else, Tom was an over-achiever from day one. His mother proudly remembers her son ferociously playing hockey with older and much bigger youths. "Tom was so fast they couldn't keep up with him," Mary Lee remembers proudly. "One guy got so exasperated he picked Tom up by the scruff of the neck and seat of his pants and moved him outside the boundary."

Off the rink, life was even more chaotic and downright dangerous. Tom was a self-described loner with very few friends. Childhood, he has said, "was very pressured, very difficult. I didn't have many friends. I think it made me self-destructive. I was very self-destructive when I was growing up. I was reckless. I'm still that way, but in a more specific way. My recklessness goes into the work." Indeed, his is a productive recklessness that has led him to pick risky roles like a paraplegic in *Born on the Fourth of July*.

His youthful recklessness, however, was more often unpro-ductive, sometimes disastrous. "Back then I was always looking for attention. I'd get into fights, get suspended from school. I think it was out of a need to be creative," he has said.

Even goofing around after school was risky business. Still it elicited from Cruise total concentration and the goal of being the best. When an acquaintance invited him over to try out his new motorbike, Tom accepted the invitation, then lied he knew all about motorcycles when in reality he had never even ridden on the back of one. Like the quick study he would later become on movie sets, he closely watched the other youths operate the motorcycle's throttle and clutch. Finally, it was his turn. For once, the quick study hadn't done his "homework." Thinking it was the brake, he twisted the accelerator located in the bike's handlebars. The motorcycle promptly crashed into the side of a house, with Tom still on it. As he later said sheepishly, "I nearly killed myself trying to be one of the guys."

Somehow, you get the feeling Cruise doesn't keep high school yearbooks around for those lonely moments when he's feeling nostalgic. More than likely, he'd keep those mementos if he were preparing to play a clinically depressed character in yet another stretching role. "I look back upon high school and grade school, and I would never want to go back there. Not in a million years." And to date, he's kept his promise. Glen Ridge High's most famous son has never been back for a back-slapping ceremony to honor him.

Cruise's athletic workaholism ended in disaster. To lose a single pound and make his weight class on the wrestling team his senior year, he ran up and down a flight of stairs—until he tore a tendon in his leg, which permanently ended his athletic career.

But like so many other apparent disasters in his life, Cruise managed to make lemonade out of lemons. Sidelined from the wrestling team, he decided to try out for his high school's production of *Guys and Dolls*. And foreshadowing his later rapid rise in the movies, he landed the starring role of Nathan Detroit, the proprietor of a floating crap game, played by Frank Sinatra in the 1955 film version.

A sidelined jock turned star of the class play, Tom should have been ineluctable babe bait. He certainly tried. Like most teens, he was vain about his appearance, and his compulsiveness about this and any other endeavor took over. He refused to eat after 5 P.M. to keep off the baby fat that is still visible in his films that don't call for a muscled look (*Risky Business, Born on the Fourth of July*). And he pumped iron with the mania of a Schwarzenegger in high school.

But even with his buffed bod and, well, movie-star good looks, Tom kept the girls at arm's length. His shyness toward the opposite sex came from an insecurity which he would forever overcompensate for by being the best at whatever he did, except seduction.

"I was scared to death of being rejected [by girls]," he has said. "And I was shy unless I got that look or that smile. But after that, I could talk to girls easily because I was close to my sisters."

It wasn't just with women that Tom felt a paralyzing shyness. He was wary of both sexes. He has admitted he didn't make many friends as a teenager, and he remembers being lonely and withdrawn, a youth who didn't express his feelings. "Traveling the way I did, you're closed off from a lot of people," he has said. "I never really seemed to fit in anywhere."

The family's modest socio-economic status in the affluent community may have also crimped Tom's style as a wannabe Lothario. A female friend recalled that he once bragged to her that he would be a "millionaire by age thirty." The boast in retrospect turned out to be modest, since he would achieve his monetary goal a good seven years earlier!

In 1989, *People* magazine would herald him on its cover as "The Sexiest Man Alive," joining the ranks of other studs like Mel Gibson and JFK, Jr., but in high school he felt more like the geekiest kid on the block. "I never felt particularly good-looking. I thought my smile was off," he said, ironically describing one of his greatest assets as a matinée idol.

In fact, his "look" was so powerful that years later a movie mogul would call on the Cruise physiognomy to beef up a cartoon character. Disney's production chief, Jeff Katzenberg, was obsessing over the fact that the title character in *Aladdin* wasn't handsome enough. Katzenberg ordered a glossy of Cruise tacked to the office wall of the film's head animator. Every day, as the artist hunched over his drawing board, he was supposed to gaze on Cruise's face for inspiration. The not so subliminal message must have sunk in because *People* magazine noted that Aladdin did indeed look like Cruise's cartoon twin.

But all this homage in cels was years away. His lack of self-confidence in his physical attributes, however ill-founded, may explain why he had only one girlfriend in high school. And this relationship wasn't very serious. It was definitely not love or even puppy love, because years later he would confide to a reporter that the very first love of his life was Rebecca De Mornay, his *Risky Business* co-star. Tom was twenty-one when he made his first big hit, and it's revealing that he didn't fall in love during the hormonal avalanche of adolescence. He was a full-grown man before the love bug bit.

Even so, he still enjoyed the attentions of women, without giving away his heart. He is a man who is genuinely fond of the opposite gender, not necessarily as sex objects but as friends and confidantes. He attributes his feelings about women to growing up in an female household. "To most men," he said precociously at age twenty-one, "women are this mysterious breed, and once a month strange things happen to them. I grew up with sisters, and I saw how they dealt with everything. After the divorce, my mother worked three jobs to hold the family together and keep us clothed and send us to good schools. My mother didn't have a college degree, and I was very sensitive to the way men treated her at work and how she handled them." If nothing else, Cruise is a younger version of Alan Alda, the type of guy who's in touch with his feminine side.

Tom revealed one of his fondest prepubescent memories during a TV interview with Barbara Walters last year. Two of his older sisters and their friends would practice kissing boys using their brother as a stand-in. At age eight, he remembers "sprinting home from school" so these "older women" could hoist him onto the bathroom sink and smother him with kisses. "They taught me how to French kiss when I was eight years old," he recalled. "The first time I almost suffocated."

To some, these powder-room encounters might sound like child molestation, but Tom claimed to love every minute of the practice sessions, racing home every day after school to attend "classes" in the lessons of love—or at least lessons in open-mouth kissing.

A few years later, Cruise would metamorphose from kissing kid brother to fierce protector. When a busboy at a restaurant looked at his sister with apparent lust in his heart, Cruise pulled him aside and snarled, "You son of a bitch! You touch my sister and I will kill you."

During another interview, for *US* magazine, a reporter asked him to recall his worst and best moments from childhood. Typically, he claimed he couldn't think of anything bad. His happiest moment, however, suggests a work ethic that would later make him excel at every endeavor, whether it was acting, racing cars with the ability of a professional driver, or taking hard punches for a fight scene.

It also suggests the family's poverty and young Tom's uncanny ability to always ferret out the gray cloud's hidden silver interior. One Sunday, he bicycled five miles to put his ten cents down on a hot fudge sundae at a local ice cream parlor. The dime had come from odd jobs, and Tom remembered that the confection tasted particularly delicious because he had *worked for it.*

He didn't say what after school job had enriched him enough to splurge on a ten-cent sundae, but if it was mowing lawns, then he indeed had reason to be gratified. "When I cut the grass as a kid, I had to achieve the goal of the best yard in the neighborhood," the perfectionist once said.

Years later, that same perfectionism would prompt an actor friend to say admiringly, "Tom wants to be the best at everything he does. It doesn't matter if it's tiddlywinks, racing a car, or being a movie star. He's going to be the best. That's his number one goal."

The family fortune and finances received a dramatic boost when Tom was sixteen and his mother remarried. Tom's new stepdad was Jack South, a plastics salesman. Accounts of his relationship with his stepdad, whose economic status allowed them to move to a nicer house, vary according to the source. Even Tom's own recollections slalom from one end of the spectrum to the other.

"In the beginning, I felt threatened by my stepdad," he has said. His greatest fear was losing his preeminent position as man of the house and cynosure of his mother's undivided attention.

A high school friend later claimed that South was something of a wicked stepfather, but other contemporaries paint a more convivial picture of life with stepfather. They remember that Tom and his new father would bet on football games. Jack was such a poor prognosticator that Tom earned more money from these wagers than mowing lawns or delivering newspapers. Another friend described Jack South as "kind and affectionate."

Tom himself offers the highest praise of his surrogate dad. "All my values and motivations really come from my stepfather," he has said.

Contrast that encomium with his bitter assessment of his biological father's abandoning the family after the divorce: "When I was older I realized I missed that certain kind of love, motivation, sense of self that comes from having a father. But at the time I didn't stop and say, 'My dad's not around. I've got to learn how to handle it.' I just felt very insecure."

Even when his parents were still together, his strongest recollection was of an absentee dad. "My father was not a guy to go out and hit baseballs to me. It was my mother who took me to my first ball game," he recalled bitterly.

Jack South's plastics job required his new family to move to Glen Ridge, New Jersey, after Tom's sophomore year.

At Glen Ridge High his teachers still remember the earnest

young man fondly despite the incessant interview requests from reporters and biographers. Dr. Marcia Bossart, superintendent of public schools in Glen Ridge, says wearily, "They get calls from the press constantly."

Glen Ridge High's greatest claim to fame may not simply be its most successful alumnus. The school was also the place where the acting bug first bit Tom Cruise. It was an "infection" that lasted a lifetime.

After the poverty, the dislocation of frequent moves, the injury that kept him away from his beloved athletics, the stage was a safe place for the lonely young man to come out of his self-imposed cocoon. And the butterfly that emerged was an instant star.

His mother and stepfather attended opening night of *Guys and Dolls* with their son in the second lead. Supportive as always, his mother applauded lustily and later remembered that night with the same enthusiasm she felt then. "I can't describe the feeling that was there. It was just an incredible experience to see what we felt was a lot of talent coming forth all of a sudden."

It wasn't just understandable maternal bias. An agent in the high school auditorium called Tom a "natural" and went backstage to urge the seventeen year old to turn pro.

Tom had had two game plans for after graduation: hitchhike all over Europe, then join the Air Force and become a real-life top gun. After essaying Nathan Detroit and earning praise from his parents and professionals, Tom decided against the grand tour of Europe and a career as a flyboy. (Ironically, his make-believe stint as an aviator would turn him into a bona fide superstar six years after abandoning plans to join the real thing.)

If acting is indeed a bug that can bite you, Cruise was overwhelmed by the virus. It was a terminal case of "I love acting."

As he would later recall, emotions and pride he had never felt before suffused him on stage in a moment of epiphany. If not a star, at least a dedicated actor was born that night in Glen

Ridge. "All of a sudden you are up there, and you're doing something you really enjoy," he said, recalling that night. "And you are getting all this attention, and people who never turned their heads or said anything before are now saying, 'Gee, look at him!' And I said to myself, 'This is it!' As soon as I started acting, I felt from that point on that if I didn't go for this, I would be making a terrible mistake." As his later career decisions would prove, Thomas Cruise Mapother IV rarely makes mistakes.

Tom was so certain he had found the right career path he skipped high school graduation to rush to New York to make his mark as an actor.

He only had $500 in his pocket, but he was enriched by the enthusiastic blessings of his mother and stepfather. Mary Lee later said that she and her husband supported Tom's decision one hundred percent. "We felt it was a God-given talent. We gave him our blessing... and the rest is history," she has said.

Arriving in the Big Apple in 1980, his success was almost instantaneous. It's a phenomenon that would be a hallmark of nearly all his endeavors, on and off the screen.

# TWO

# New York, New York

Cruise's early days in the theater capital weren't much different from any other struggling actor's. He bussed tables, unloaded trucks, and did janitorial work in his apartment building in return for a reduction in his rent. Unlike other wannabe thespians, however, Cruise's days as a struggling actor were literally that—*days*.

Within a few weeks of hitting the city, he landed the role of Herb in a dinner theater production of *Godspell* in Bloomfield, New Jersey. So it wasn't David Mamet at the Shubert, at least it wasn't unplugging toilet bowls in his apartment building.

And there were setbacks along the way. On a visit to Los Angeles to audition for the TV version of the movie *Fame*, a casting director said Cruise was "too intense" for television. The casting exec was probably right about that, but he was dead wrong when he added that Cruise wasn't "pretty enough" either. Adding insult to injury, the man suggested Tom get a tan while he was in L.A. so the trip wouldn't be a total loss.

Another actor might have given up at this point and gone back to school to become an accountant or a junior high school teacher, but not Tom Cruise. Once he maps out his goal, he zeroes in on it and doesn't let up until he has achieved it. Proof is in the fact that despite his *GQ*-model looks, he is an unlikely movie star. First of all, he's too short at 5'7". And his voice is that of a pipsqueek. His dyslexia must make it impossible to do cold readings when auditioning for a part, although he hasn't had to undergo that humiliation since his first monster hit, *Risky Business.*

An associate marvels, "Tom has the concentration of a brain surgeon—or a great athlete. Once he sets his mind to something, watch out! He'll move heaven and earth—and a movie studio, which is considerably heavier—to get what he thinks is right. He doesn't demand superstar perks. He's not one of those childish stars who wants his Winnebago on the set repainted because the color depresses him. I've known stars who've made idiotic demands like that, stars who act like members of the royal family and insist on being treated that way. Not Tom. He's 'just folks' with a hundred million dollars."

Setbacks like *Fame* were easily forgotten when after only five months in New York he got a small role in Franco Zefirelli's *Endless Love,* a hankie soaper about teen angst starring Brooke Shields. At seventeen, Cruise was unable to sign the film contract himself and was forced to bring his mother along to co-sign in his manager's office. "Can you imagine how embarrassing that must have been?" says an observer. "He must have felt like a five year old whose mother accompanies him to school the first day of kindergarten. Whew!"

His embarrassment would soon be compounded by anger. The manager had a demeaning habit of summoning her young protégé to her office, telling him she had an important deal to discuss. When he got there, she'd have him run errands, pick up dry cleaning, and even do her grocery shopping!

After a month of this abuse, he told his manager he planned to fire her. She shot back that he couldn't because he was under contract to her for the next five years. Like the legal sharpie he would later play in several movies, Cruise told the woman that since he had signed the contract underage, it wasn't legally binding.

"Thank God," he would later say with a sigh of still tangible relief, "I was only seventeen." The industrious young man hired a lawyer to break the contract and soon got another manager who had better uses for his client than errand boy.

"Tom doesn't make outrageous demands, but he does demand to be treated with respect. Even when he was a nobody, a struggling actor, he still demanded respect, but not in a pushy way. He just let you know he was a guy who had feelings too, and you better not trample on them," says a long-time acquaintance.

Eventually Cruise dropped the manager who replaced his first one. He felt self-sufficient and confident enough to manage his own career. Later he would dispense with the services of a money manager as well and make all his investments personally.

"Managers," he once said determinedly, "can be a Hollywood trap." Many older and presumably wiser stars have been ripped off by unscrupulous managers and "investors to the stars." Cruise's impoverished childhood had taught him the value of a dollar, and he wasn't about to let someone else spend those dollars for him, even though the money would eventually amount to hundreds of millions.

"Tom is not cheap, but he's a holy terror if he feels you're taking advantage of him," says a colleague. "Despite the dyslexia, he's quite bright, and if you work for him you have to stay on your toes. Actually, you have to run to keep up with him. He's a force of nature, the sort of guy whose actions say, 'Lead, follow, or get the fuck out of my way,' although he'd never put it so crudely. I've never heard him utter an obscenity for all the years I've known him. He's always the perfect gentleman, even in the locker room."

*Endless Love* was not a propitious omen for Cruise's future success as a major player in the movie industry. In fact, the only thing memorable about the film is that a then unknown by the name of Tom Cruise had a microscopic part in it. *Endless Love*'s most notable contribution to the cinema may be its function as a question in Trivial Pursuit.

Designed as a showcase for Brooke Shields, this sappy vehicle almost drove her career into the ground. In the early 1980s, Shields was hot, but not for her acting ability. In Marshall McLuhan's words, she was famous for being famous. Shields had enjoyed some critical success as a child prostitute in *Pretty Baby*, and she demonstrated her box-office clout in critically reviled commercial hits like *The Blue Lagoon*. Still, at this point in her career she remained an unknown quantity. Was she a genuine actress or was she just another screen novelty, like Pia Zadora or Bo Derek? *Endless Love* would definitely answer that question, much to Shields's chagrin.

The critical abuse *Endless Love* received suggested that the beautiful Shields should stick to modeling in those endless jeans ads, where nothing came between her and her Calvins. Unfortunately, Shields refused to see the writing on the wall—and the barbs in the press—and she continued to star in flops, each one more embarrassing than the previous one. (Remember *Sahara* or *Brenda Star*?)

Martin Hewitt, the male lead in *Endless Love* enjoyed an even less exalted pedigree than his teeny-bopper co-star. The film's director, Franco Zeffirelli spotted him parking cars at a restaurant in Pasadena and decided to give the handsome unknown a starring role in a major studio release. Zeffirelli explained his unusual casting choice by describing the handsome unknown as "like a small bull, but with immense charm." If Lana Turner could be discovered at the soda fountain at Schwabs, Hewitt might as well be discovered in a parking lot looking like a miniature cow.

Fortunately for the future superstar, Cruise's role in the film was so tiny he was listed eighteenth in the cast credits. His presence in this deplorable mess was so slight—a total of seven minutes on screen—that it didn't hurt his career.

Despite the dreadful end result, the film is notable for a number of cast members who, unlike Shields and like Cruise, went on to future glory. Way above Cruise in the credits was somebody named "Jimmy" Spader, who would evolve into a more mature sounding James Spader, the star of the classic film about yuppie impotence and masturbation, *sex, lies and video-tape*. Even further down in the credits was Ian Ziering, who would later attend high school for seven years on *Beverly Hills 90210*.

In his cameo debut, Cruise was cast as a psycho high school student named Billy, who comes up with the lame idea of setting fire to Brooke Shields's house so that Hewitt can then rescue her and become a hero. Hewitt takes Cruise up on his suggestion. But the fire spreads too rapidly, and Shields's family is almost killed in the holocaust. Molly Haskell in the *New York Times* described Hewitt's character as "Holden Caulfield as arsonist." If only the film had as much class as *Catcher in the Rye* or even the popular cult novel by Scott Spencer on which *Endless Love* was tangentially based. (The novel was set in the '60s, and Shields's parents were hippies. By 1981, when the film was made, the '60s hadn't yet become nostalgically chic, and a major thematic element of the novel—the Vietnam War years in America—was lost when the story was updated to the present. Somehow, the Reagan decade of greed just didn't have the same resonance as the flower-power setting of the novel.)

It's amusing that both in his debut film and his next project, *Taps*, casting directors seemed to single out Cruise for psycho roles. With his boy-next-door looks, especially that grin, you would think he would have been typecast as, well, the boy next door, not the pyromaniac down the block or in his next film, the psychotic cadet down the dormitory hall. It may have been Cruise's intensity, which would serve him so well in his later films, that caught the eye of casting directors. The casting people may have also decided to cast the fresh-faced youngster against type. Whatever their reasoning, these casting agents knew what they were doing by plucking this unknown out of obscurity and giving him his first two film roles. Later in his career, Cruise would use his intensity in the service of good-guy roles. But while he was paying his dues in bit parts, he would show that he could play against his leading-man looks.

Director Zeffirelli can take credit for discovering the future superstar. The Italian director said, "I went through hell and paradise looking for kids to fit my visual impression." (One wonders what Zeffirelli saw in Cruise's fresh face that made him instantly think "psycho arson.")

As written, the role superficially tapped into Cruise's optimistic attitude toward life. His character, Billy, was a *cheerful* psycho who recalls with glee that when he was eight he set fire to the neighbors' house and became a hero after alerting them to the blaze. Hewitt is inspired by this story and decides to burn down girlfriend Shields's house. Unfortunately, Hewitt doesn't have a way with a match the way Cruise does, and he burns down the whole house. Instead of being a hero and winning the approval of Shields's parents, he's sent to prison.

Although this may be after-the-fact Cruise lore, Zeffirelli reportedly kissed his fingertips and purred, "Bellissimo," after Cruise auditioned for the theatrical filmmaker, who directs operas in his spare time. This anecdote sounds more like myth-making after Cruise became a superstar, since he only had seven minutes on film. It's hard to imagine what kind of emoting Cruise could have done in such a tiny role to elicit such a dramatic response from the director.

Cruise was a wannabe film actor at the time, but he was obviously no film student. The teenager hadn't even heard of Zeffirelli, despite the fact that the director had made such hits as *Romeo and Juliet* and *The Taming of the Shrew.* Ignorance is bliss, at least in this case, since Cruise was able to audition for the director without feeling nervous about being vetted by such a major movie talent.

The neophyte actor in retrospect must have considered himself lucky that no one associated him with *Endless Love.* The cinematic soap opera became the butt of jokes, with the *Los Angeles Herald Examiner* reporting that there "was howling in the aisles" of the theater during a preview screening of the film. "For the last fifteen minutes of it," one witness reported, "the audience just howled." This would have been good news for a Mel Brooks movie, but disastrous for the melodrama Zeffirelli had meant to direct.

*Endless Love* was such an embarrassment for all concerned, the publicity machine at Universal, which produced the tearless-jerker, tried to distance itself from the film it was supposed to be promoting. Everyone was having such a good time making fun of Shields and her film, even the head of publicity at the studio got in on the act of badmouthing the movie. "Well, there's only one place to put the blame," Gordon Armstrong, Universal's vice president of hype, said, "and that's on the word-of-mouth. The promotion was perfect," he added, covering his hide.

Cruise may have initially been disappointed that his role was so tiny, but after the annihilating reviews came out, he may have been glad that his role was so miniscule no reviewers deigned to mention him in their diatribes against the principals.

*Endless Love* contains an amusing factoid that should appeal to trivia buffs and people with a macabre sense of humor. The film was almost assigned to Paul Schrader, the director of such kinky films as *Cat People*, *Hardcore*, and *American Gigolo*. Until a series of flops slowed his career, Schrader loved to make films about fringe people, like Robert De Niro's Travis Bickle in *Taxi Driver*, which Schrader wrote. With Schrader at the helm of the sappy *Endless Love*, you can almost imagine him downplaying the romance between Shields and Hewitt and zeroing in on the psychotic teen played by Cruise and his sexual fascination with fire. It would have been a completely different film, and Cruise's prominence in it could have killed his career before it got off the ground. (Look what it did for Martin Hewitt's.)

The ambitious youngster had given himself three years to find work as an actor. Instead, he achieved the goal in five months! As one Cruise-watcher commented, it would be the last time the actor underestimated himself! Tom was definitely on the fast track in the film industry.

Still, *Endless Love* only paid scale, about $300 a day at the time, and he only worked one day on the film. When he auditioned for his next film, *Taps*, he literally didn't have a dollar to his name. So he hitchhiked home to New Jersey to await the call from his agent. When the call came telling him he had the bit part, Cruise became so excited, he later recalled, "I smashed my head on the door frame!"

His talent on the set stood out immediately. Originally cast in a tiny part, Tom got his first break when the director reluctantly decided to fire the actor who had a major role as a psychotic cadet. Impressed with Tom's intensity, he offered the much larger part to the novice.

Typical of the code of honor which has influenced so many other career decisions, Cruise at first refused to take the job away from a colleague. But when the director explained that the other actor was going to get the ax regardless of Cruise's decision, Tom threw himself into the bigger role.

*Taps*, a well-received drama about cadets who take over their school when it's threatened with closing due to budget cutback, was more than a major step up in his career. He made lifelong friends of his co-stars Timothy Hutton and Sean Penn.

The film also gave him real money for the first time in his life. Cruise remembered feeling like a kid in a candy store—or more accurately, a starving actor in a surf & turf restaurant.

In the present era of anorexic teens, Tom's deprived childhood stands out in stark contrast. Back then, he couldn't afford to be a finnicky eater because one of his sisters would have snatched the food away from her dawdling brother. As he remembered, "I ate *a lot*. Growing up I always ate what was on my plate, and sometimes there wasn't enough food. So it was like the person who finished first got that extra piece."

*Taps* gave him a lavish *per diem* allowance for meals, $100, standard for all union film productions. It wasn't standard for the once hungry actor. He splurged. Every night after shooting, he'd invade an expensive steakhouse and stuff himself with filet mignon and lobster. It was the first time in his life he had ever tasted the pricey shellfish, and he enjoyed this small taste of the good life with somewhat unfortunate results. "I must have put on ten pounds," he said ruefully.

In 1981, *Taps* also saw the emergence of a typical trait that afflicts many actors who enjoy early success. It's even given rise to the term "Brat Pack." As Cruise described the phenomenon himself, "After *Taps*, I became an asshole. I was the most unpleasant person to be around. My family even said, 'Look, cut it out, take it easy, buddy!' But I've learned from my mistakes, and that kind of stuff has just gone away."

Before learning those lessons, he cut quite a path—literally. During a break on the set of *Taps*, the former overachieving mower of lawns jumped on a lawnmower and chewed up the finely manicured lawn on the grounds of the military academy.

# THREE

# Lost in Tijuana

After *Taps*, a big-budget, big-star outing, Tom Cruise made what to many might seem like a stupid career move. In 1982, he signed to star with another relatively unknown by the name of Shelley Long in a no-brainer, low-budget, teen exploitation comedy originally titled *Tijuana*.

Eventually, a marketing decision was made to change the title to *Losin' It*, a double entendre intended to capitalize on all the teen exploitation films that were cleaning up at the box office during the early '80s with titles like *Zapped!* and *The Joy of Sex*. The new title referred to the characters' virginity, which Cruise and two friends hoped to discard in Tijuana.

The decision to star in *Losin' It*, however, wasn't totally crazy. After *Taps*, Cruise rightfully feared that he would be forever typecast as a tightly-wound psycho. *Taps* had been his first major role, and it was the only measure by which directors and producers could judge his talent.

So many other promising young actors and actresses have found themselves playing variations on their first successful role and ended up in the "Whatever happened to...?" file. *Losin' It* was a chance to prove he could play light and carefree, that the psycho cadet could do sex farces, that a pyro pervert could light up the screen with something other than a four-alarm fire.

If anyone had predicted that the star of *Losin' It* would one day be the number one box-office attraction in the world, he would have been committed to the Home for the Terminally Optimistic.

While marketers wanted to capitalize on the youth market by giving *Losin' It* its naughty-sounding name, the film was more than naughty. Although teens were the obvious target audience, the film had so much heavy-duty carnality it earned an R rating, which on paper at least was supposed to keep those under seventeen out of the theater unless accompanied by an unfortunate adult. The producers and the studio were probably demonstrating supreme cynicism when they didn't order the film recut for a more commercial PG rating—it was the industry's dirty little not-so-secret that theater owners were routinely ignoring the R rating stipulation and letting anyone in who could reach high enough to give the ticket taker the price of admission.

In its review of the film, which wasn't a *total* pan, *The New York Times*'s Janet Maslin described the future matinée idol as a Jerry Mather look-alike. The defunct *Los Angeles Herald-Examiner*'s Peter Rainer, who now skewers films for the *Los Angeles Times*, more accurately described the movie as "an attempt to do *Porky's* in Tijuana."

*Porky's* was the defining tits-n-ass movie of the period, and other critics couldn't resist damning comparisons. The *Village Voice*'s Andrew Sarris called it "another sample of the Porky the Penis genre" and marvelled over the innocence of the period (the early '60s) and the teenagers' naive belief in the existence of Spanish fly, a pivotal plot point in the film.

The film's bordello scenes must have caused the upright young actor a moral dilemma. Later, when he had clout and could pick and choose any role he wanted, Cruise would choose not to take on overtly sexual films like *Indecent Proposal* or drug dramas like *Rush* and *Bright Lights, Big City*. But in 1982, with only two films under his belt, Cruise had to swallow any moral qualms he might harbor for the sake of advancing his career, although at the time appearing in such a witless outing must have seemed like anything but an advance.

*Losin' It* is one of those small films like *The Lords of Flat-bush* that employed several unknowns (Sylvester Stallone, Henry Winkler) who would later become big stars. *Cheers*, which would make her the bluestocking cocktail waitress you loved to hate, was still at the bottom of the Nielsens, and Shelley Long, a minor sitcom actress at the time, did some slumming in the film as a bored housewife who teams up with the three teenagers. While *The New York Times*'s review didn't even deign to identify Cruise by name (only mentioning his character's resemblance to the title star of *Leave It To Beaver*), the reviewer did single out Shelley Long "who demonstrates impressive talents as a physical comedienne."

The first-time director of this mindless fun would also go on to bigger projects and much bigger stars. Curtis Hanson would direct Rob Lowe in his semi-autobiographical (Lowe's not Hanson's) *Bad Influence*, then score a huge hit with *The Hand That Rocks the Cradle*. The bad taste left in the director's mouth by exploitation films like *Bad Influence* and *Losin' It* must have been completely expunged by his latest collaborator, Meryl Streep, whom Hanson directed in her first action film, 1994's *The River Wild*.

Cruise prefers to dismiss *Losin' It*, but in his typically sunny outlook he also manages to find something good about the experience. "*Losin' It* is an important film for me. I can look at it and say, 'Thank God, I've grown,'" he has said.

The Z-list talent in front of and behind the camera on *Losin' It* (Shelley Long hadn't become a star on *Cheers* yet because the low-rated show was almost cancelled after its first season), taught Cruise the importance of picking one's collaborators wisely and well. "I realized that if you want to grow as an actor, you have to work with the best people. Then you'll be able to have more control over what you do," he said in retrospect.

Even at the age of twenty-one, it's interesting that Cruise, an unknown with virtually no clout, was already obsessing about control. But at this point in his young career he was too inexperienced to realize that the more talent and success your co-star or director has, the more control he can exercise and the less you can. It would be years before Cruise was able to put his philosophy into practice and work with the "best people" like Paul Newman and director Martin Scorsese. And by then, he had learned how to finesse older, more established colleagues by treating them with such deference and near idolatry that they didn't realize they were being flattered by their savvy younger associate.

In *Losin' It*, he would have to put up with mediocrity and the resulting mediocre product, a mindless teen sex farce.

During an interview for another film, a reporter mentioned that she had seen *Losin' It*. Cruise wanted to know if she had paid to see it, and the reporter said yes. Demonstrating the self-deprecating wit which endears him to journalists, Cruise whipped out a $20 bill to compensate the interviewer for wasting her own money on the turkey. Since movie tickets in the early '80s when *Losin' It* was released only cost about $4, the additional $16 may have been for "damages."

After *Losin' It*, Cruise joined the cast of another small film for which he would have to make no apology even though it was not a commercial hit. Unlike *Losin' It*, his next project would be directed by one of the major filmmakers of all time with a canny knack for casting unknowns who would later become major players in the acting fraternity. Just as Francis Ford Coppola had discovered an older generation of greats like Al Pacino and Robert De Niro in his *Godfather* sagas, the director now tapped a cast of new faces whose names would later resonate in the pages of *Variety* and *People* magazines.

# FOUR

# Greaser Glory

For the 1983 black and white film about working class youth called *The Outsiders*, Coppola hired Matt Dillon, Ralph Macchio (*The Karate Kid*), Patrick Swayze, Rob Lowe, and Emilio Estevez. In more melodramatic and dangerous terms, the plot of the film echoed Cruise's own modest upbringing surrounded by upscale teens. Matt Dillon plays a young punk who leads a gang against a preppie clique at their high school. It was the greasers vs. the socs (pronounced "soshes," as in social sophisticates).

Almost unrecognizable, the twenty-one-year-old Cruise played a greaser with a chipped tooth who worked at a gas station. His character's name was Soda Pop.

Tom pumped up for the role, proudly rolling up the sleeves of his stained T-shirt to show off his newly developed biceps, complete with a tattoo (unpermanent). He also got into method acting in a way that must have made him less than a joy to work with, especially in close-up scenes. Like Nick Nolte as the homeless savant in *Down and Out in Beverly Hills*, Cruise didn't bathe for the duration of the shoot!

Although he later claimed he abandoned his "asshole" ways shortly after *Taps*, there was enough of the devil in Tom to join in the pranks the cast played on one another. Tellingly, Tom, however, chose such relatively harmless gags as scrawling "Hel-ter, Skelter," on co-star Diane Lane's makeup mirror. By con-trast, Emilio Estevez lived up to his reputation as the founding member of the Brat Pack by tying a bag of feces on Tom's door-knob and smearing honey on Lane's toilet seat.

Not surprisingly, these youthful cutups didn't escape the censure of the press. In a famous *New York* magazine article, David Blum dubbed these twenty-something actors on the cusp of stardom the "Brat Pack." As the monicker suggests, it was not a flattering article, and Emilio Estevez, who figured prominent-ly in it, was furious. His close friend, Ally Sheedy, says Estevez insisted he had been set up. He didn't really hang out with all those so-called Brat Packers.

The journalist who coined the term asked Estevez to round up some fellow actors, and they all had dinner at the Hard Rock Cafe in West Hollywood. Dinner conversation revealed them to be promiscuous, contemptuous of women, and immature. Estevez was disdainful of the waitress who served them. When a Brat Packer told her a friend had just passed the bar exam, the waitress said, "I didn't know you had to take a test to become a bartender." Interestingly, although Cruise is now a charter member of this age group of actors, he did not appear at the notorious dinner and wasn't even featured in the article.

"Brat Pack" was a clever if irrelevant term that conjured up images of the wilder "Rat Pack" of thirty years earlier. The Rat Pack gang was a collection of actors and singers that included Frank Sinatra, Dean Martin, Sammy Davis, Jr., Peter Lawford, and occasionally his brother-in-law, then Senator John F. Kennedy. On and off, Marilyn Monroe and Shirley MacLaine, among others, served as members of the female auxiliary of the Rat Pack. Their "frat house" was Vegas, a perfect place for these mostly married men to play away from home and wives.

The Brat Pack was more a fictional creation of a journalist with a great knack for coining a memorable phrase than a cohe-sive group of actors who hung out together. Even if these young men weren't pals, the ground-breaking article revealed the self-absorption and cockiness of a group of good looking guys just out of puberty with the money and clout usually enjoyed by older men.

The term gained even greater resonance because it came to describe a movie genre that would dominate much of the '80s. The film industry catered to all those baby-boomer ticket buyers just reaching their twenties. Hence, theaters were bombarded with twenty-something-themed movies, usually of the tits-n-ass variety with casual alcoholism and drug use thrown in for laughs.

The Brat Pack designation didn't stick to Cruise for long. It was largely his doing that kept him out of the clique and the genre. As he told me, "When I was starting out, there was a whole trend of youth films. I had to pace myself. I didn't want to be identified with that kind of movie."

He quickly surpassed his peer group, proving in a series of well-crafted films he could be more than a teen heartthrob with a winning smile. His coevals didn't fare as well. A group photo of the male cast of *The Outsiders* is revealing—and a little sad. All the handsome young men in the publicity still would go on to have one hit—or two at most—then lose their career once their teenage looks deserted them and they began to look their age. In amusing greaser attire, the cast photo shows Emilio Estevez, Rob Lowe, C. Thomas Howell, Matt Dillon, Ralph Macchio, Patrick Swayze, and, scowling, still in character, Tom Cruise.

That was then.

This is now: Estevez, a promising actor, has found himself forced to capitalize on one big hit, *The Mighty Ducks*, and endure a less successful sequel.

Rob Lowe would go on to star in home videos, but not the kind you can rent at the local video store.

C. Thomas Howell. Who?

Matt Dillon has followed up his Brat Pack years with some

impressive performances. Unfortunately, they were all in movies that didn't do well at the box office, thus limiting his crack at the A-list scripts, which are routinely offered to his one-time peer, Cruise.

Ralph Macchio had one great role as *The Karate Kid*, then found himself playing the same kid into his thirties in two sequels.

Of the group, excluding Cruise of course, Patrick Swayze would enjoy the greatest post-*Outsiders* success with two blockbusters, *Ghost* and *Dirty Dancing*. His career would then follow the same downward spiral that afflicts so many teen heartthrobs, who have the longevity of a tse-tse fly when they can no longer rely on their looks and have to summon up real talent.

Cruise escaped this Brat Pack curse. As Paul Newman accurately predicted, "Tom may be the only survivor" of the group.

Coppola didn't care what a reporter chose to call his young actors, especially Tom Cruise. The director was so impressed with Cruise's performance in *The Outsiders* that as soon as filming was completed, he immediately offered the young unknown a bigger role in his next project, *Rumblefish*.

Once again demonstrating an almost psychic ability to pick hits, Cruise had the chutzpah to turn down the director of *The Godfather* to appear in another teen exploitation film with a director who had never made a film before! Cruise's crystal fiscal ball didn't fail him. *Rumblefish* was a box-office flop. The teen sex comedy he chose would make him a superstar overnight!

# FIVE

# Not So Risky Business

O n paper, the storyline for *Risky Business* doesn't sound much loftier than *Losin' It*: An affluent teen turns his home into a brothel while his parents are away on vacation and in the process gains admission to Princeton!

Even with a can of the film *Losin' It* under his arm, Cruise found a lot of resistance from the producers to casting him in his breakthrough film. It was his too-convincing performance as a psycho cadet in *Taps* that had lodged itself in the consciousness of the filmmakers that kept getting in the way. "They didn't even want to see me for *Risky Business*," Tom later recalled with a shudder. "The director had seen me in *Taps* and thought I was this lunatic with a shaved head."

When he finally got in to see the director, Tom had totally transformed his looks with long greasy hair and a wispy beard. It wasn't the right look for an affluent Chicago teenager—the role in *Risky Business*—but it did demonstrate that he could metamorphose into something totally different. His transformation must have paid off. Entertainment mogul David Geffen, whose production company made the film after every studio in town had passed on it, took a chance and cast Cruise in the starring role.

Cruise was virtually an unknown prior to *Risky Business*. There were many other actors in his age group much better known and better box-office draws like Emilio Estevez and Matt Dillon. Except for *Losin' It*, a little-seen, low-budget film, all of Cruise's film roles had been minor supporting characters.

To entrust the lead in a major studio release to an unknown is rare in the overly cautious film industry. Sometimes a studio will cast an unknown in one lead if the other lead is famous, such as Goldie Hawn and Armand Assante in *Private Benjamin* or Kathleen Turner and John Laughlin in *Crimes of Passion*. But Cruise's leading lady was Rebecca De Mornay, who had even less experience and a smaller film profile than her leading man.

Geffen's gamble paid off. And it made Tom Cruise the new teen heartthrob, a certifiable movie star at the precocious age of twenty-one.

More ominously, *Risky Business* also gave the first hint of what would become known as "Cruise Control," the actor's obsession with controlling all aspects of a production. At this point in his career, Cruise Control was subtle and helpful. His suggestions actually enriched the production.

Early in the film, Cruise's neurotic parents go out of town on vacation and leave strict instructions with their son not to throw any parties in their beautifully appointed home. A great deal of the film's fun comes from the way Cruise's character, Joel Goodsen, totally ignores their command and goes way beyond hosting parties and turns the place into a suburban whorehouse in the middle of pricey Winnetka. The locale (wealthy suburbia near Chicago) and theme (teen runs amuck) sounds like a John Hughes film, only R rated.

During his first night without parental supervision, Joel's idea of a good time is pretty tame and gives no indication of what's to come. He eats, or tries to eat, a frozen TV dinner without defrosting it.

And then comes the scene that helped the little comedy earn a big $65 million. The stage directions in the script simply said, "Joel dances in the living room." It was Cruise's inspired idea to dance in the living room in his underwear. The actor also came up with the music (Bob Seger's "Old Time Rock and Roll") and the choreography, which has Joel playing air guitar while he dances.

It was a magical moment, and its impact was due to Cruise's new-found talent as a script doctor. Years later, his script doctoring would lead to conflict with an Oscar-winning screenwriter and the unfortunate choice of several cookie-cutter movies, but for the moment Cruise had nothing but great ideas.

The image of Cruise dancing in skivvies became so iconic that years later the son of the President of the United States, Ron Reagan, a professional ballet dancer, would recreate the scene for a sketch on national television—in his underwear.

Rev. Jimmy Swaggart, at the time a well-known televangelist and Christian Right advocate, denounced the *Saturday Night Live* sketch. Although President Reagan was quoted in the press as saying he thought his son's network appearance in underwear was all good clean fun, Swaggart claimed he had personally talked to the leader of the free world, who told him he was shocked and scandalized by his son's BVD-ing all over the small screen.

The original scene, Ron Reagan's parody of it, the national attention it caused, and Swaggart's hypocritical denunciation of it, were all generated by Cruise's clever script doctoring. ("Joel dances in the living room.") When he was finished mouthing the uninspired stage directions he transformed them into a classic movie image as indelible as Bogart's good-bye to Bergman at the airport in *Casablanca*.

Rebecca De Mornay's supernal beauty also created many memorable moments—mostly sexual—in the film. De Mornay played a teen prostitute. It is her professional expertise that

helps Cruise turn his sumptuous suburban home into a prosper-
ous whorehouse.

Cruise was a big booster of the actress and her performance
in the film. "I love the way Rebecca played her part, because she
didn't do the happy hooker. There was sadness and reality. She
asks, 'Why does it always have to be so tough?'"

As it turns out, in fact, the very first love of Tom Cruise's
life was Rebecca De Mornay, his *Risky Business* co-star. "There
were girls you like a lot, but I'd never been in love before. Since
I've been with [Rebecca], it's opened me up a lot," he said. "I
think it's helped me be a better actor. I was pretty lonely. I was
really lonely before I met her. Rebecca is so strong and honest.
I'm already a better person and a better actor because of our
relationship," he added during the full blush of their romance.

Contrary to Cruise's squeaky clean interpretation of De
Mornay's interpretation, *Risky Business* is a variation on the
happy-hooker theme. De Mornay's hooker is sophisticated,
wears beautiful clothes, and seems in control of her life. That is
the same kind of rosy view of prostitution that *Pretty Woman*
peddled into $200 million and the number one box-office hit of
the year. There was minimal "sadness," to use Cruise's term, in
the masturbatory fantasy that many critics believed *Risky Business* was. As for being reality-based, Cruise was such an innocent, he didn't realize that there was a seamy side to
prostitution, like drug addiction, abusive pimps, and prison
time. De Mornay, not to mention the writer/director of the film
Paul Brickman, made selling one's body for cash look glamorous
rather than ugly.

There was nothing ugly about two ultra-erotic love scenes
between the hooker played by De Mornay and Cruise's high
school student: one on the stairs of the house, the other in an
empty subway car.

One critic said with a mixture of awe and revulsion,
"Those scenes verge on pornographic. You practically felt there
was penetration going on out of sight of the camera lens. It was

amazing to see what was basically a fuck film with a major studio budget. If the film had been shot on videotape, it would have looked like any other pornographic movie except that the stars were a lot better looking than most of the dogs you see rutting around in porno flicks."

The only problem for Cruise was that, at first, he wasn't turned on by De Mornay. A method actor, he felt the lack of chemistry between them was seriously impeding his performance. And although he was not a star yet, he had the temerity to demand that De Mornay be fired!

"He just felt that she wasn't very good," remembered one insider. "Even though he claimed to have fallen in love with her later."

How far Tom had come from refusing to take his fired colleague's role in *Taps*. But Cruise wasn't a star yet and didn't have the clout to make his wishes stick; he was just another up-and-coming actor expected to do what he was told. But that didn't stop him from pestering the film's genial producer, Steve Tisch, who told him point blank to work around his aversion to De Mornay.

Cruise demonstrated his professionalism in spades. Not only did he overcome the lack of combustion between them, he moved into De Mornay's hotel room!

Tisch learned about this transformation when Cruise told him he didn't need an allowance for housing anymore. Rebecca's suite would suit them both nicely.

The steamy eroticism of the stairway and subway scenes suggest that Cruise's "sacrifice" was well worth it. At the age of twenty-one, when most of his peers were still hustling tips in restaurants, Cruise had become a force in the movie industry.

*Risky Business* writer/director Paul Brickman's stylish comedy earned rave reviews and, more importantly, $70 million when it was released in 1983.

*Newsweek*'s film critic, David Ansen, perfectly summed up the film's ability to go beyond the greasy kid stuff of this genre.

"*Risky Business* is not just another youth comedy, although in outline it may sound like the forty-seventh horny-teenager's-sexual-initiation movie of the year. A brief synopsis doesn't begin to suggest what Paul Brickman's fresh, hypnotic and very sexy movie feels like…It's a dreamlike version of a boy's sexual awakening."

The usually acerbic *Village Voice* added its hosannas: "*Risky Business* demonstrates that no genre, however rundown, is beyond redemption by just a little wit and talent."

Cruise may have bedded his leading lady for the sake of a good performance, but their intense affair lasted more than two years. Overcoming his inexplicable physical aversion to the beautiful young actress—maybe it was her offbeat Brigitte Bardot looks—Tom discovered a greater bond with De Mornay than the carnal. To this day Cruise refuses to discuss the relationship.

Years later, after the affair was over, the actress, who is more open than her famous ex-lover, would speculate on the source of their strong emotional ties. De Mornay's parents also divorced when she was young, and to this day she remains estranged from her father, right-wing TV commentator Wally George. "There's definitely something different about kids who come from broken homes. They have this sort of searching quality because you're searching for love and affection if you've been robbed of substantial amounts of time with your parents. I think that's true of Tom," the actress has said.

In fact, Cruise was robbed of almost all time with his absentee father. However, unlike De Mornay, who has never reconciled with her dad, Cruise at least enjoyed a sense of completion and reconciliation on his father's death bed.

# SIX

# Life With(out) Father

**B**efore his father's death in 1984, Tom had come to terms with all the suppressed rage he felt about the man who had abandoned the family and left his wife and children scrounging for food stamps and hand-me-downs. "I forgave him," Tom said simply.

It was Tom who sought the reconciliation, and it was Tom who had to locate his father. His determination in tracking him down was provident since the older man was dying of cancer. Somehow, however, Tom learned of his father's condition and tracked the man down to his hospital room.

He was surprised and rewarded for his persistence. "I think there are things about me that are like my father. I was surprised because I hadn't seen my father for a number of years. I heard he was dying, and I didn't know where he was," Cruise recalled. "He didn't *want* to be contacted. He left and didn't want to be contacted for years. I think he was tired of inflicting so much pain on other people that he just had to get away."

To this day, Tom refuses to let bitterness over his father's behavior overwhelm him. He has his father's own misery as a cautionary tale. "I think my father made so many mistakes it ate him alive. Even when I went to see him, he didn't want to discuss what had occurred in the past."

Polite as always, Tom didn't press his father for a deathbed confession of all the sins of omission he had committed against the family. "I said, 'Whatever you want, dad.' But I held his hand. And I told him I loved him and that I was going to miss him. He said when he got out of the hospital we'd go have a steak and a beer and talk about it then. He died before we could do that."

Cruise's memories of life with his father weren't all bad, but even the happy recollections are tinged with a hint of a household where violent discipline was the norm. The actor remembers getting close to his father for a brief time, but their male bonding was abruptly interrupted by his parents' divorce.

"My father wasn't around very much," Cruise said. "I love my father, but he'd come home at six o'clock and we'd sit and watch Walter Cronkite and then *Batman* on television. Then he'd go back to work or it was time for us to go to bed…As a kid, you're kind of afraid of your dad because he is the guy who usually comes home to punish you and beat the hell out of you and send you to bed with no dinner. I didn't get to know my father better until later. When I was about ten years old, for about one year, we got real close. But then he and my mother got divorced, and I didn't see him for a long time."

Cruise still refuses to pat himself on the back for absolving his father on his deathbed. He remembers his own impetuous days as a young adult, his self-described "asshole" years, and somehow found it in himself to forgive his dad for what sounds like a lifetime of "asshole" years.

"Fifteen years ago I was a moron," Tom confessed recently. "I was in confusion. I was angry about it. All the things you've got to take responsibility for in your life, it makes forgiveness quite easy."

Still, you get the feeling Tom sorely missed paternal encouragement. When friends later told him that his father was enormously proud of his son's success, Tom morosely replied, "He never told *me* that."

His father never did get to see a single one of the films that had made his son a national icon. Gamely, the older man tried to get out of his hospital bed and catch a matinée of *Risky Business*, but he was too ill to leave his room. These were the days before home video.

Graciously, Tom refused to put *all* the blame on his father for the years-long rift. As he told a counterculture London magazine, *Time Out*, "It wasn't just a one-sided responsibility, me not speaking with him or him not speaking with me. It's much more complex than that." Unfortunately, the reclusive actor was not more forthcoming and didn't elaborate on the complexities of this tortured father-son relationship.

Still, in the same interview, he couldn't keep from letting a bit of the bile spill out of his usually closed-mouth approach to granting audiences with the press. "Would I have liked a happier childhood and a loving father? Would I have liked to have had it differently? Maybe I wouldn't be where I am today if it had been. There are no accidents. I don't know, but I don't like pain just like anybody else doesn't. I feel it."

That last meeting in his father's hospital room was the stuff of movie dramas. Perhaps sometime, after the painful memories have receded, Cruise (the wannabe director) will make a film about his troubled non-relationship with his father.

His father died before Tom's next film came out, and maybe it was a blessing. In fact, Tom's next two films suggested his early success was a fluke and that he would soon be joining the ranks of other one-hit wonders.

His first film after *Risky Business*, 1983's *All the Right Moves* (which, in terms of box-office and critical acclaim, might have more appropriately been called *All the Wrong Moves*) suggests an artistic cautiousness he would later mercifully abandon.

*All the Right Moves* was something of a *Risky Business* clone that transferred the setting from upscale Chicago to a hard scrabble Pennsylvania mining town. Unlike his affluent Joel Goodsen in *Risky Business*, Cruise played Stef Djordjevic, a lower-middle-class youth desperate to escape his town's poverty. (It was a bizarre name for a movie character and so unpronounceable the studio felt obliged to include a phonetic spelling of Stef's surname, presumably, in case anyone wanted to discuss the film out loud.)

Stef Djordjevic (pronounced "Georgia-vitch" per the helpful folks at Fox) was a role closer to Cruise's own socio-economic background than *Risky Business*'s Ivy League-bound pimp. Like the real Tom Cruise, who escaped his roots by dint of hard work and talent, the hero of *All the Right Moves* could only hope to move up the economic ladder by winning a football scholarship to college. Joel Goodsenn got into Princeton by making passes at hookers; Stef Djordjevic had to make passes with footballs.

As one critic complained, *All the Right Moves* was a variation on the theme of *Risky Business* only not nearly so stylish or entertaining. The public agreed, and Cruise's first film outing after the huge success of *Risky Business* looked as though it might be his last.

Although *All the Right Moves* did nothing for Cruise's career, it did help out the town where the flop was filmed, Johnstown, Pennsylvania. In 1983, Johnstown suffered from the worst unemployment rate in the entire country. The decaying town was a perfect microcosm for the dead-end life Cruise's character Stef faced.

The residents of Johnstown were overjoyed by the invasion of a free-spending movie crew, and the love affair lasted almost two months. The severely depressed economy suddenly found itself showered with 2,800 jobs for local residents, including work as extras and ancillary jobs. More than $2 million was pumped into Johnstown, which sorely needed the injection.

As Cruise looked at the townsfolk, eager to earn their $45-a-day salary as extras, he must have reflected on his own much happier fate, which could have easily been that of the unemployed inhabitants of the dying steel town.

The employment of 2,800 locals, unfortunately, didn't begin to put a dent in the town's unemployment, even temporarily. Johnstown's biggest employer, the Bethlehem Steel Corporation, had laid off five thousand of the plant's seven thousand workers by the time the film company arrived in town.

Although the Hollywood invaders spent lavishly, $300,000 on hotel accommodations and dinners alone, the production company was stingy when it came to the locals. For the movie's climactic football game, the town's sixty-year-old Point Stadium was packed with townspeople working as extras—for free. They didn't even get the $45 *per diem* that a film company shooting in Southern California and covered by the Screen Extras Guild contract would have been required to pay. A local newspaper, however, cheerfully reported that the producers did offer extras free soft drinks, hot dogs, and raffle prizes.

The film is noteworthy for several bits of movie trivia. It has the genuine distinction of being the only film in which Tom appears with black hair. The perfectionist actor noticed that in certain light the camera caught auburn highlights in his hair. Cruise wanted everything about his character to say bleak and grimy, so he dyed his hair to reflect the grim steel town.

*All the Right Moves* also had the distinction of being the first feature film produced by Lucille Ball, whose company also created *Star Trek* and the TV series which will soon be adapted as a feature-film vehicle for Cruise, *Mission: Impossible*. Trivia buffs may be more interested to know why Ball's name doesn't appear in the credits. The late comedienne's husband, Gary Morton, explained, "I took Lucy's name off because it's R rated." A columnist wrote that after the failure of the film, Lucy might be grateful it wasn't on her resumé.

*All the Right Moves* almost capsized Cruise's career. The *Village Voice's* Andrew Sarris even predicted Cruise had already used up his fifteen minutes of fame from *Risky Business* and that *All the Right Moves* "should probably set him back to square one."

But beautiful women were not keeping such close tabs on his box-office track record or withering notices. The sexy teen from *Risky Business* had lodged in their collective consciousness, and Cruise was irresistible babe bait.

Although he claimed his success at the time turned him into a temporary "asshole," his behavior during this period suggests he was being too hard on himself. The code of ethics, including honesty inculcated in him by his mother and stepfather, stopped him from turning into a young clone of Warren Beatty.

Graham Greene said fame is a powerful aphrodisiac, and there's nothing like the fame of movie stardom to encourage somewhat brazen groupies. Sean Penn related one incident that is perhaps typical of the way Cruise handled such situations.

A beautiful woman approached Cruise in a bar and told him pointblank, "I want your body!" According to Penn, Tom freaked out and screamed at the would-be groupie, "I have a girlfriend I'm in love with."

The woman, who was more interested in a one-night stand, didn't care what his motivation was and shot back, "You should have told me that five minutes ago."

Unlike Beatty and other Hollywood Lotharios, Tom Cruise was and still is a one-woman man. His faith in fidelity was so strong that years later when it came time to leave the first Mrs. Cruise to take up with the second, he would wait until he had been formally separated. Sexual integrity like this is rare—practically nonexistent—among Hollywood's handsome leading men, who practically have to step over the bodies of willing groupies to get to the set.

Cruise has said that the pain of his parents' divorce on his mother and her children has made him wary of marriage. And when it finally did come time to get a divorce, he wanted it to be for more compelling reasons than a one-night stand with a star-struck groupie. It would take more than casual sex to propel him toward the painful dissolution of a marriage.

At this juncture in his life and career, however, the young actor had more serious things to worry about than those that go bump in the night. If he kept picking the wrong projects like *All the Right Moves*, pretty soon there wouldn't be any groupies to fend off.

*Legend*, Cruise's next film choice, was made for all the wrong reasons. As an adult, he still had warm memories of his childhood love of fairy tales enriched by his affection for the teller of those tales. "As a kid I liked fairy tales. My mother used to read them to me. When (director Ridley Scott) told me the story, I really wanted to a be a part of it. It was a physical challenge."

Tellingly, Cruise apparently signed on to the project based on a director's enthusiastic oral pitch and Ridley Scott's reputation as a stylish creator of fantasy universes like *Blade Runner*'s."

Had his dyslexia made him postpone actually reading the script of this story about a youth searching for a unicorn in a mythical universe?

*Legend* had more problems than a soporific script and overlong running time. With only ten days to go in principal photography, the giant soundstage at Pinewood Studios burned to the ground. The fire represented more than the loss of *Legend's* soundstage. Described as the largest movie soundstage in the world, the set at Pinewood had been used for three James Bond films, beginning in 1976 with *The Spy Who Loved Me*. The fire in this historic set was so intense, smoke could be seen from five miles away. Two stagehands and four firemen were treated for burns, smoke inhalation, and shock. Fortunately no one was seriously hurt. With the delay of rebuilding the intricately designed forest where the unicorn and Tom forlornly romped, the hot young star found himself wasting an entire year of his life shooting this battle ax of a movie. Cruise could have dropped out of the project after the fire, but he stuck with it, despite the fact that by then it was obvious *Legend* would not be a legend on his resumé. His agent even offered to help him break the contract.

Cruise later explained that the death of his father shortly before starting the film made him feel a lack of completion in the relationship. He misguidedly sought a sense of completion from the film instead.

*Legend* not only helped him deal with the loss of his father, it also kept him so occupied he didn't have time to brood over his father's death. "I don't know what I would have done without my work," he later explained. "It gave me a place to deal with all those emotions." Or more likely, the backbreaking schedule of fourteen-hour days on a movie set allowed him to sublimate his father's death into the job at hand, starring in a very complex film.

His relationship with Rebecca De Mornay was still hot and heavy after *Risky Business* and during the *Legend* shoot in London. Even the Atlantic couldn't keep these young lovers apart. De Mornay traveled to London several times during filming at Pinewood Studios to be near Cruise.

To play the mythical hero, Cruise let his hair grow down to his shoulders. He joked, "Now my hair is longer than Rebecca's. Sometimes I wash it and clean the bugs out of it." Later, preview audiences would laugh when they saw what looked like a hippie version of the teenaged pimp from *Risky Business* running around the enchanted forest. The young girls in the audience, Cruise's main constituency, criticized what they described as a "pageboy haircut."

When De Mornay returned to the US, Tom would take solitary strolls in London's Hyde Park. The drizzle and fog of the city must have compounded his depression and sense of loss. Psychologists say that the death of a parent, especially the death of a parent of the same sex as the child, reminds the child of his own mortality. At the ripe old age of twenty-three, Cruise felt a little bit of himself die with his father.

Besides dealing with his father's death, Cruise had to put up with some ugly business on the set. One scene called for Tom, who played Jack O' the Green, to cradle a baby fox in his lap. Although the creature was only a few weeks old, it had a mean streak. While the cameras rolled, Cruise stayed in character instead of screaming out in pain because the fox was using the star as his personal scratching post. The fox shredded his leg, which began to bleed. But Cruise didn't complain while the animal slashed his million-dollar legs.

Trouper that he is, Cruise insisted on doing most of his own stunts, with disastrous results. After performing a series of death-defying somersaults for another scene, Cruise pulled a muscle in his back and spent the rest of the three-month shoot limping in pain.

Stoically, Cruise never complained about the pain. He was so cooperative that the director couldn't contain himself when describing their happy professional collaboration. "For him to do this movie is very brave. As a career step it's very challenging. Suddenly he's stepping out of the usual kind of role that a twenty-three-year-old guy is going to do and into a much more theatrical situation. He coped with it wonderfully, and his enthusiasm and commitment were unusual," Scott praised.

The director also managed to tone down his star's style of acting, which at the time lacked subtlety. With Scott's gentle coaching, Cruise learned to rein in his emotions while the camera was recording them. It was a talent he would use to much greater effect on *Born on the Fourth of July*, which required him to display the gamut of emotions, not just the silly, sexy grin which had served as his signature trademark on previous films.

*Legend* came out and flopped noisily in 1986.

Universal, which produced the film, didn't know what to do with this turkey and apparently panicked. The original score, which Oscar-winner Jerry Goldsmith spent six months composing, was unceremoniously dumped and replaced with music by Tangerine Dream, a synthesizer rock band from Germany that had previously scored *Risky Business* and *Firestarter*. Goldsmith's score was based on Elizabethan music and perfectly suited the Old World flavor of the film. Tangerine Dream's space-age use of a Moog synthesizer would have been better suited to a sci-fi adventure rather the medieval setting of *Legend*.

Scott lamely explained the score change by saying, "I wanted parents to have something to take their children to, though the film is aimed at all ages." The $30-million film's box-office take of only $10 million suggested that neither children nor their parents were interested, regardless of the score.

The studio also cut twenty minutes from the European version of the film before its later release in the US, shrinking its running time to only ninety minutes. But the executives were wasting their time with all this last-minute surgery; nothing could save it. While the boys in the Black Tower (Universal's executive building near downtown Burbank) fretted about how to retool *Legend* into a viewer-friendly film, they postponed it from its planned June 1985 release, when it would have been up against summer blockbusters, and practically sneaked it into theaters during the lull of April the following year.

Even the normally genial second-string film critic for the *Los Angeles Times*, who never met a film he didn't love, hated *Legend*. Thomas, who was the only critic to put *Heaven's Gate* on his ten-best list of the year, suddenly turned on the industry and wrote, "According to Ridley Scott, legends are born of the eternal struggle between the forces of light and darkness. Perhaps so, but it's hard to imagine his legend living up to its name … *Legend* has even less substance than Scott's last film, *Blade Runner*. *Legend* seems a distillation of all the illustrations for all the fairy tales ever read to a child." Tougher critics said the film was more like a nightmare than a fairy tale.

The *Chicago Tribune*'s Gene Siskel, who has been labelled a "popcorn critic" for his low-brow tastes, hated *Legend* even more than his colleague at the *Los Angeles Times*. "Having to write this review is akin to recalling a bad dream," Siskel wrote.

The counterculture *Village Voice* compared the film to a bad acid trip.

Another critic found at least some good in the film's failure. Its box-office performance killed once and for all the movie genre known as sword and sorcery, which included stultifying "action" films like *The Keep* and *Conan the Barbarian*.

All these negative reviews took their toll on the star, who did something very unlike himself. The normally controlled young man went berserk, and, according to a reputable British magazine, trashed his hotel room.

It's an image of the star that's hard to imagine: The unfailingly polite, extremely self-controlled workaholic going on a rampage. This *volte-face* in his usual behavior suggests Cruise cares even more about winning than observing proper decorum in a luxury suite in London. Still, somehow the sight of Cruise acting more like a rock star trashing a hotel room than a superstar granting royal-like audiences to a fawning press is hard to conjure.

Cruise could have saved himself the wear and tear on the hotel furniture—if he did indeed trash his room—if only he had known that his next movie would make everyone forget the disaster of *Legend*. And it would transform him from movie star to movie icon, the most bankable actor in Hollywood.

# SEVEN

# Top Dog

For all his commercial savvy and position atop the box-office hill, Tom Cruise is not greedy. Earlier, when he wasn't making a million dollars per picture, he still turned down a lucrative commercial endorsement for Ray-Bans, the brand of sunglasses he put on the map in *Risky Business*.

As the idealistic star later explained, "I'm an actor and not into that kind of stuff. Money is seductive, but I didn't become an actor for the money. The money isn't why I work. It's great to have, though," says a man who makes $15 million per picture plus a cut of the gross, not the net, income.

And even more costly to his bank balance, the twenty-four-year-old Cruise originally turned *Top Gun* down flat despite its promising pedigree. The decision showed a lot of integrity and guts, although some thought "nuts" was a more appropriate description of his behavior.

*Top Gun* had two of the most successful producers in Hollywood, Don Simpson and Jerry Bruckheimer, at the helm. Although the producing pair have fallen on hard times recently at Disney, back in 1986 they were hotter than Mount Saint Helens. They had produced *Flashdance*, the two *Beverly Hills Cops*, all blockbusters.

Cruise didn't care about the Simpson-Bruckheimer track record or the step up in his career that *Top Gun* could and eventually would provide. It was those pesky ethics of his that kept getting in the way. Maybe that single year in the seminary still had a lingering effect on his moral code. (Years later he would turn down a slew of future hits like *Indecent Proposal* because they either glorified drugs or promoted, well, indecent sexual behavior.)

Just as Cruise could self-righteously turn away a beautiful groupie in search of a one-night stand, he could just as easily turn down a $1-million fee to star in a film that he thought was just as morally bankrupt as taking advantage of a star-struck fan.

Cruise felt the original script for *Top Gun* glorified war and killing. Jingoism was not something he felt comfortable promoting, no matter what the paycheck.

Unlike his status on *Risky Business*, when he didn't even have the clout to ax an unappealing co-star, the superstar now had enough power to exert the beginnings of his notorious Cruise Control. He imperiously ordered the two top producers in Hollywood to commission a major rewrite of the jingoistic, gung-ho script.

Cruise wanted to downplay the murder and mayhem and focus on the camaraderie of the Navy pilots. By now he had the power to transform John Wayne-type hokum into a more palatable buddy picture that just happened to involve the deaths of unseen enemy pilots who were disposable Libyans to boot.

For once in Hollywood, morality had a financial payoff. It was the back-slapping, skirt-chasing, bar-singing, volleyball-playing jock aviators who made *Top Gun* a success, not its now submerged militaristic message. (Even so, after the film came out, the Navy reported a feeding frenzy of young men signing up to live Tom Cruise's film fantasy.)

But even after the film was rewritten to the star's specifications, he still balked. Producer Don Simpson played his trump card. Like a spider welcoming the unsuspecting fly into its web,

Simpson pulled some strings to allow Cruise to take a ride in an F-14 jet.

This did the trick. "I realized going in that the movie was going to get hit from people thinking it was a right-wing military movie," he said after its release. "But what excited me about the movie was the planes. I *love* planes! I saw the movie as *Star Wars* with real aircraft. It was a nice E-ticket ride, a simple movie but involving."

He did indeed love planes. Simpson claims that as soon as Cruise emerged from his rollercoaster ride in the sky, he signed on to make *Top Gun*. "When Tom hit the ground," Simpson recalled, "he said, 'I'm in!'"

Cruise was thrilled by the high-flying experience. The military advisors on the film were not so thrilled with the actor who was representing them on screen.

One Naval officer claimed that Cruise had to wear what the macho servicemen call "pussy patches." These are cousins of those proliferating nicotine patches, but instead of slowly secreting nicotine into the wearer's blood stream, pussy patches infuse anti-nausea medication at a steady rate. The officer later said, "You know if I had photos of this guy, Tom Cruise, white as a ghost and ready to puke his liver out, I'd be a millionaire. I think from there on in, Tom had to wear pussy patches." It seems that the risk-taking superstar experienced recurring nausea aboard the F-14. Another advisor said in an interview that Cruise was "incredibly vain." That vanity included the star's demand that he appear in the volleyball scene without his shirt in order to show off his recently buffed bod. "Cruise was incredibly straight-laced, focused, and businesslike," one crew member recalled. "He wanted to make a lot of money. He was also extremely vain. He cared about how he looked." The crew member added, "The volleyball scenes were added to show some flesh."

The film's director, Tony Scott, didn't object to his star injecting beefcake into the movie. In fact, Scott remembered

Cruise as being exceedingly polite, almost excruciatingly so. "Tom is frighteningly polite," Scott said. "He's so nice he's sick." Scott remembered Cruise calling a fan who asked for an autograph "Sir," even though the fan was about his age.

Despite all the flesh on the beach, it was, after all, male flesh. And while that might have been enough to bring in the female audience, male moviegoers needed something more to get them panting. At least that's what the filmmakers thought.

After principal shooting was completed, the producers and director Tony Scott immediately saw that there was something seriously missing on screen: any inkling of combustion between Cruise and his leading lady, Kelly McGillis. An advisor on the set said, "There was never any chemistry between them. But he was much too proper a gentleman to say anything bad about her." Cruise had obviously come a long way from the days when he tried to get Rebecca De Mornay fired because she didn't turn him on and was seriously hurting his performance in the sex scenes.

There were no love scenes in the original cut of *Top Gun*, so it didn't bother the actor that McGillis was even less his type than De Mornay had been. But it was painfully evident in the editing room that Cruise and McGillis just didn't have the hots for each other.

That was soon remedied. At enormous expense, the crew and the two stars were reassembled to film an R-rated nude scene at McGillis's beachfront home in the movie.

We can only imagine how uncomfortable this R-rated addenda made the young actor feel. For by his own admission, he is an old-fashioned prude. "Love scenes make me nervous. It's very strange to get in bed with someone you don't really know. They're embarrassed, and I'm kinda going, 'You OK? Right then, let's do it.'

"It's no fun at all. You have to be professional about it. You respect the other person's feelings. There's a line you don't cross. I don't [cross that line], and it's never been done to me."

The liberal film community and the equally liberal press that covers it wasn't impressed with *Top Gun*'s alleged watering down of the jingoistic content. *Time* magazine harumphed, "He takes suicidal militarism and makes it sexy."

The public didn't care about the film's subtext. Fans wanted to join Cruise on this E-ticket ride, and they did so in droves. To date, the film has pulled in almost half a billion dollars!

*Top Gun* was the number one box-office champ of 1986. It grossed more than $170 million in the US and Canada alone. Action films like *Top Gun* do even better overseas, so double the $170 million figure to calculate the adventure flick's worldwide take. You can be sure every covetous studio executive in town was doing the same arithmetic.

But the gross from the theatrical release of the flyboy flick was only the beginning of the bonanza that started rolling into Paramount's coffers. After an eight-to-nine month tour of theaters worldwide, films have a second life in video release. Later, there's the airing on pay cable. Finally, the TV networks get their shot. When it's announced that a film grossed "x" number of dollars at the box office, that's just the tip of the fiscal iceberg. Triple that figure due to video, cable, and network showings, to determine a film's real booty.

Is it any wonder that a few years later the National Organization of Theater Owners (NATO) named Cruise Star of the Year at its annual ShoWest convention in Las Vegas, which the eager-to-please superstar dutifully attended to pick up his award? In terms of career longevity, a NATO accolade means more than an Oscar. Meryl Streep owns matching Oscars. Tom Cruise doesn't have any. Guess which star the studios would rather make a picture with?

"It's impossible to exaggerate the kind of clout starring in a half-a-billion-dollar grosser like *Top Gun* gives the star of the movie," says an industry insider. "He or she gets first crack at all the best scripts—even those that are grotesquely unsuited for the superstar. If the role doesn't quite fit the big name actor who wants it, the studio is only too happy to retool the script to the point of being unrecognizable from the writer's original version on paper.

"The studio brass don't care if the writer is grossed out by this. They can always hire another more compliant writer to tailor-make the script for Mr. or Ms. Big Box Office. Did you ever wonder why the credits for so many films list two or more writers?

"The reason usually is that a second, or even third writer (or in the case of *The Flintstones* half the membership of the Screenwriters Guild) is dragooned into retrofitting the script so that an inappropriate casting decision becomes perfect casting."

The incredible popularity of *Top Gun* marked the closing of one chapter in the young actor's life and the opening of another, one he wasn't thrilled about. Before *Top Gun* made him the aviator women would most like to fly with, Cruise was just another up-and-coming actor with one big hit to his name. After *Top Gun*, he went from film star to movie icon. *Top Gun's* high profile meant the end of his cozy anonymity. That's the only thing, it seems, that Cruise doesn't like about his success.

"I used to be able to walk around, but after *Top Gun* I'm recognized everywhere," he lamented after the film's opening. At that time, the actor promised he wouldn't turn into the male Garbo, a transformation he would later make with the help of his press agent. Back then, he said, "I refuse to change my lifestyle. I don't *not* go out because I'm afraid or have bodyguards or any of that kind of bull. It can be frightening when people are all over you. But you just have to relax. I try to be as polite as possible. If you run, they're going to chase you; look at Newman. He deals with it very well. I can learn a lot from that."

Unlike Sylvester Stallone, Cruise doesn't employ bodyguards, nor does he have an entourage, an accessory so many other superstars feel they need. At movie premieres, you can always see him alone, except for his wife. And instead of bodyguards at public appearances, walking a few feet behind her client, like a bride at a Japanese wedding, is his press agent, Pat Kingsley.

Jerry Bruckheimer, paraphrasing Frank Sinatra's estimation of his own popularity, cited the reason female *and* male fans love Tom Cruise. Bruckheimer said, "Guys want to be like him and girls want to be with him."

Besides superstardom, Cruise also found another father figure/mentor to replace his absentee dad in the unlikely person of Don Simpson. One of Cruise's self-improvement tasks involved hanging out at Simpson's office and raiding his library. Simpson told *Time* magazine, "He comes into my office and goes over my stack of books, taking notes. Last night he used the word 'plethora'! Two years ago he didn't know the word."

Cruise may have needed to look up the word after it was used to describe his film's box-office receipts or maybe the thousands of fan mail letters that inundate his agent weekly.

Indeed, 1986 was a watershed year for Tom Cruise. *Top Gun* cost a piddling $15 million and earned more than the gross national income of some South American countries. The film also proved that he could carry a picture on his own. He was a box-office smash.

The normally grumpy Roger Ebert, one of the most powerful film critics in the country, gushed, "With *Top Gun*, Tom Cruise ascends into the stratosphere of movie stardom." *Life* magazine called him a "magnet for women." NATO named him box-office star of the year, shutting out other big moneymakers like Sylvester Stallone, Eddie Murphy, and Paul Hogan, who had all had big hits that year as well. And for a man who claimed he didn't care about money, his asking price shot up to $10 million per picture after he climbed out of the fighter jet.

But the post-release euphoria of *Top Gun* was nothing

compared to an even more monumental event in his private life. At a dinner party the confirmed bachelor who had said he would never marry because of his own parents' painful divorce met the woman who would make him change his mind about wedlock.

# EIGHT

# The First
# Mrs. Cruise

A t that point in her career—1986—it's hard to pin-
point Mimi Rogers's exact place in the firmament of
stars. She was too far into her career to be called a
groupie, yet she wasn't far enough along to be called
a star. Starlet is the term that comes to mind, although even that
wannabe designation doesn't do justice to the status she had
achieved. It's just that all her starring projects up to that time
were flops. Unfortunately for her and her marriage to the
world's number one movie star, her track record wouldn't
change after she became Mrs. Tom Cruise.

Cruise was instantly smitten by the statuesque, well-
endowed actress, who, like his current wife, towered over him.
Unlike many men, Tom apparently doesn't object to being the
"junior" partner in a relationship, stature-wise. He was also her
junior chronologically; he was twenty-four, Mimi thirty-two,
when they met. Like many other men who enjoy early success—John Travolta and Pierce Brosnan come to mind—Cruise
preferred more mature women who matched his emotional if
not actual age.

In fact, Cruise was so well known for preferring older,
taller women that one myth became enshrined in fact. Many
reputable publications casually reported that Cher and Cruise
were an item. It sounded plausible. Cher is famous—infa-

mous—for preferring younger men, and Cruise liked older women. It would have been a perfect match of boy toy and mature nurturer. But it just wasn't true.

In 1986 *Vogue* printed a brief item that explained how rumors take on a life of their own and become "fact" or "factoids", in Norman Mailer's terms. When Cher broke up with her genuine boy toy, twenty-nine-year-old network executive Josh Donen, she moved out of their Manhattan co-op and sublet the unit to Cruise—alone. When Cher reconciled with Donen, she wanted her co-op back, and Cruise graciously vacated the premises. Cruise was Cher's tenant, not her lover or even one-night stand.

Other movie-star romances were vehemently denied by his then publicist, Andrea Jaffe. When an item appeared that Cruise and his *Top Gun* co-star Kelly McGillis had been spotted necking furiously in the back of a public movie theater, she issued a vigorous denial that the two stars were romantically trussed.

It's easy to see why Cruise fell in love with Rogers. She was and is gorgeous, although like his first love, Rebecca De Mornay, Mimi has slightly offbeat looks. Her lantern jaw was slightly crooked, giving her smile a loopy tilt. Men—and movie cameras—found the bemused expression created by her lopsided lips irresistibly sexy. One journalist even made an overwrought comparison to Mona Lisa's enigmatic grin in describing Rogers's.

Rogers disagreed. No one could accuse the actress of being narcissistic about her looks, which she described like this in an interview: "I have a completely irregular face. My mother was a totally gorgeous blonde Southern babe from North Carolina, and my father was a Jew from Detroit. My features are completely out of whack. I need a front-end alignment," she said.

As her later nude pictorial in *Playboy* would show, she also has a great body. But it wasn't her physical allure that struck the ascetic superstar first.

"This woman is extremely bright," he later remembered thinking when he met the curvaceous actress. Cruise was right about that. She graduated from high school, where she excelled in math and science, at the Doogie Howser-ish age of fourteen, after having skipped not one but two grades during her shortened formal education.

Her scientific aptitude had probably been inherited from her father, a civil engineer, who had worked on Dulles International Airport. Her artistic bent came from mom, a dance and theater major in college.

These two beautiful people first connected at an intimate dinner party, which had only ten lucky guests. Cruise got a chance to set his sights on Rogers in close quarters: "She sat right next to me. I thought she was very bright, very sexy, very easy to talk to," he recalled. "We just had a lot in common, including the same sense of humor. We had lots of laughs."

Although Rogers's childhood, like the second Mrs. Cruise's, was much higher socio-economically, the two were soulmates on a more profound, psychological level.

Like Cruise, Mimi came from a broken home. Her parents divorced when she was seven. Besides being children of divorce, both Tom and Mimi were children of the road. Mimi's father got custody of his daughter and her brother. Every year the family moved to a new city. Rogers later called her father "the original wandering Jew." And like her future husband, Rogers learned how to be a quick study, fitting in wherever her father's new job took the family.

Tom Cruise and Mimi Rogers were married May 9, 1987.

The secret of the wedding was so closely held that even his publicist at the time, Andrea Jaffe, didn't know that her most famous client was tying the knot. Only fifteen guests, mostly relatives, were invited to the nuptials, a Unitarian ceremony held in upstate New York. Tom's best friend since their work together on *The Outsiders*, Emilio Estevez, was best man. To keep the paparazzi away, the guests were only told that it would be a "spring bash." It wasn't until the guests arrived that they found they were celebrating something more momentous.

Tom's strong family ties and no-nonsense approach to luxury were symbolized by the wedding cake. It was chocolate with white marshmallow icing, and it was homemade by one of his sisters.

That the wedding even took place was something of a miracle. Before he met Mimi, Tom considered himself a confirmed bachelor. The traumatic fallout of his own parents' divorce had made him paranoid about the institution of marriage and its seemingly inevitable progression to dissolution.

"For years I said to myself, 'I'll never get married,'" Tom recalled. "You know, coming from a broken home, my worries were, 'Jesus! Am I going to be faithful? Does marriage work as a concept?' I really never thought it could."

After he met Mimi, he lost his trepidations. "I told myself, 'This is the person I really want to be with, and all the success in the world means nothing if I'm alone. We were married nearly two years ago, and I find I really enjoy marriage. It keeps you alive."

He was a devoted husband, not the Brat Pack type who would run around on his wife. "The most important thing for me is I want Mimi to be happy," he said two years after they had tied the knot.

The groom's mother was no meddling mother-in-law. Mary Lee heartily approved of her son's choice. "Mimi is exactly the kind of woman I always hoped Tom would marry. I couldn't feel more blessed," she said.

Mimi's father was as ecstatic about his new son-in-law: "I think Tom is a wonderful, warm, and caring young man. We are very happy they are married," he said.

A huge spotlight was immediately trained on the newly minted Mrs. Tom Cruise. Anybody related to the reigning superstar would have to share the often harsh glare of negative publicity, not to mention the relentless stalking of photogra-

THE FIRST MRS. CRUISE

phers, who could earn upwards of $10,000 for a single candid shot of a big-name celebrity.

The brickbats against his wife began being hurled almost immediately. A mean-spirited *People* magazine carped that Mimi was "better known for the company she keeps than for her acting career."

It was true but unkind. She had starred in two failed TV series, *The Rousters* and *Paper Dolls*. In the latter, the exotic beauty was typecast as a high-fashion model. In *The Rousters*, she was hilariously miscast as a cowpoke. *Paper Dolls* may be of interest to trivia fans because co-starring with Mimi was an unknown by the name of Daryl Hannah, who would also later gain great fame because of her connection to a famous man, JFK Jr. Mimi had also played Christopher Reeve's girlfriend in the critically acclaimed feature-film flop, *Street Smart*, and Michael Keaton's in the more successful *Gung Ho*.

It was Tom's first marriage, Mimi's second. She had been briefly married to a fellow Scientology counselor, Jim Rogers, in the '70s, when her future husband was still in high school.

After that, she had become a professional girlfriend of sorts, dating stars like Tom Selleck, ex-football player and *Hill Street Blues* actor Ed Marinaro, and American royalty like Bobby Shriver, nephew of JFK. She also became lifelong friends with another celebrity wife, Maria Shriver, sister of Bobby and wife of Arnold Schwarzenegger.

The "professional girlfriend" epithet must have rankled. In a rare public show of pique, the normally gracious actress spit out, "You have to assume there are small-minded or nasty people out there. And for some reason it makes them feel better to think, 'That little no-talent slut! She just looks for celebrities to date.'"

It was just the opposite, according to Rogers's take on this celebrity alliance. "If there was anything I was fearful would happen, it would be hearing somebody say, 'Gosh, we're really interested in Mimi for this movie...and man, Tom would really be great in the lead,'" she said. "I was armed and ready to rip out the throat of anyone who tried to do that. Even the thought of having to deal with it is humiliating."

Besides her obvious physical assets and the braininess that first grabbed him, Cruise was delighted to be married to a colleague, although a much less successful one. "It's easier. It's very helpful to be married to an actress, and Mimi is very secure in herself and very understanding. After you work these long hours, it is good to have someone who understands, who doesn't say, 'Why do you have to work fifteen hours a day? What do you mean you have to get up at 5:30 in the morning and you're not coming back until midnight?! What do you mean you've got to do *that* with a girl?'... Mimi is very cool about it," he said in the full blush of early wedlock.

Ironically, his wife's *sang froid* about her husband's long hours on the set that kept them apart may explain why the marriage eventually failed in less than three years. While Tom was away at work on his next potential blockbuster, the not-so-little woman was at home, waiting for the phone to ring from her agent.

Curiously, Rogers never appeared on screen with her husband. Maybe it was the visible age difference that made them unlikely screen lovers. She could have used some of the refracted luster from her husband's stellar career. In her one big-budget film outing, *Someone to Watch Over Me*, she showed she couldn't carry a picture on her own, and the stylish thriller directed by Ridley Scott bombed. If Tom had been superstitious, he would have warned his wife off the project, since the director was the same man who helmed one of Cruise's only flops up to that time, *Legend*.

As her husband's career flourished and hers stagnated, Rogers found her identity submerged by her mate's superstar status. The marriage began to resemble *A Star Is Born* without the booze or the great Streisand-Kristofferson soundtrack. Or, as she later said bitterly of living in the shadow of a superstar, "You cease to become a singular individual. You're never mentioned without that name. And that's hard."

Although her husband failed to impact her career positively, she had a major impact on his personal life that would spill over into the professional arena. It's an influence that for better or worse continues to this day.

One big impact Mimi had on Tom involved the Church of Scientology. Rogers persuaded her husband to attend the church's monolothic, bright blue complex, the Celebrity Centre International in Hollywood, and he's been interested ever since.

Both Rogers's parents are members of the church, and Mimi herself was a big wheel in the organization. By age fifteen she had become an "auditor," Scientology jargon for counsellor or lay minister.

Scientology is one of those new religions, like the Moonies' Unification Church, that shrouds its activities in a paranoid-like secrecy. Even if there's no wrongdoing, the secrecy itself acts like bait to the piranha press, which is determined to ferret out the cause of all the secrecy. If you have something to hide, the press's attitude seems to be, it must be because it's bad. Even the genteel *Los Angeles Times*, which usually bends over backwards to find something nice to say about everything and everyone, pulled out all stops in a series of scathing articles on the evil empire of Scientology. The *Times* claimed that church members were "brainwashed, alienated from society, punished for aberrant behavior, and were worked like slaves."

Mimi's friends have a fonder recollection of the Church. For example, John Brodie, the former San Francisco 49ers star to whom Mimi was an auditor, recalled with affection their professional/religious relationship: "There's a little something about Mimi that appeals to an awful lot of men. Everybody did better whenever she was around them. Tom Cruise certainly did."

# NINE

# Class and Crass

Whether it was the influence of Mimi's companionship, his new religion, or lucky socks, something made Cruise more productive than ever on the set. *Top Gun*, after all, proved he could turn cinematic dross into box-office platinum.

When an actor reaches superstar status with a huge commercial hit, the next thing he wants is the respect of his peers. That was one reason Steven Spielberg made *Schindler's List*—to get rid of those pesky dinosaurs and sharks that kept distracting Academy members from throwing their votes his way. For the same reason, but with much less success, Burt Reynolds got out of his souped-up car in *Smokey and the Bandit* and tried to impersonate a butch Noel Coward in *Starting Over*.

After the commercial stratosphere *Top Gun* had reached, Cruise was ready to come down out of the clouds. Like everything else he has set his mind to, from losing fat to make wrestling weight to pigging out for *Risky Business*'s pampered teen pimp, Cruise outdid himself in the search for a loftier project. He ditched crass and found class—extreme class.

He found what he was looking for in the persons of Paul Newman, something of a Tom Cruise in the '50s himself, and even more so in Martin Scorsese, one of the greatest directors of all time, heir to the *auteurist* mantle of Welles, Ford, and Hawks.

Many auteurs want to stay that way, auteurs or sole authors of their films' content and style. To that end, they avoid powerful superstars like the plague they can often be, demanding changes in scripts, often written by the director/*auteur*, to suit their whims. The best artistic directors like Woody Allen and Francis Coppola usually cast second-string stars who don't have the clout to call their agent Mike Ovitz and demand that *Manhattan* be relocated to Malibu so they won't have to fly cross-country to report to the set.

Fortunately for his career trajectory, Cruise was not yet known for his notorious Cruise Control, and Scorsese was not scared off by the powerful star. (How scary can an actor be who calls all his elders, and even some juniors, "sir" or "ma'am"?)

Tom Cruise was no Barbara Streisand, demanding full movie-star makeup when she was supposed to be playing a patient who had been incarcerated for three months in a mental hospital in *Nuts*. As he had proved before and would continue to do, Tom Cruise is the least vain actor in Hollywood. If the role required it, he was willing to shave his head or let his hair grow tangled and greasy, put on baby fat or transform himself into a pint-sized Schwarzenegger without the steroid bloat.

Fortunately for his fans, Cruise's Scorsese project didn't require him to hide his good looks or disfigure his delicate features. Later, he would go bald and play a paraplegic, but for the present film, he got to play a lower-class version of himself.

*The Color of Money* was a sequel of sorts to the 1961 classic, *The Hustler*, in which Paul Newman played "Fast" Eddy Felson, a cocky pool shark who challenges Jackie Gleason's aptly nicknamed "Minnesota Fats" for the top of the pool rack.

In the sequel, Newman was recast as the elder statesman of pool sharking, fortunately without Gleason's girth. Cruise played Vincent Lauria, the cocky claimant to the throne.

Cruise had never shot pool before. Typically, he threw himself into the art of billiards with the same obsessive perfectionism that had prompted him to pump up for *Top Gun* and pig out for *Risky Business*. He spent seven weeks prior to shooting the film shooting pool. The actor became so expert at it that not a single one of the miraculous bank shots in the film was performed by a stunt double. Cruise was too modest to mention these feats in interviews to promote the film. It was Paul Newman, like a proud papa, who revealed his protégé's legerdemain.

Cruise's relationship with Scorsese and Newman was symbiotic; the young actor wasn't the only beneficiary of the project. His box-office appeal made *The Color of Money* Scorsese's biggest commercial hit up to that time (later surpassed by *Cape Fear*).

Paul Newman got even more out of the relationship and his involvement with *The Color of Money*. The much admired actor, who had turned in bravura performances in classics like *The Verdict* and *Cool Hand Luke*, won his first and only Oscar for *The Color of Money*. (Cruise, typically, was snubbed by the Academy. He seemed to be suffering the Spielberg curse, which says that if your make a lot of money in the movie business, you don't deserve an Oscar no matter how talented you are. The Academy of Motion Picture Arts & Sciences, which hands out the statuettes, seems to feel that crass and class don't mix.)  ·

*The Color of Money* was also notable in Cruise's career because it was the first example of what would be a continuing trend in his films and choice of co-stars. From *The Color of Money* on, Cruise would often seek out older mentors who became surrogate father figures on the set. Charmed by the deferential awe he exhibits despite his own superstar status, these older actors, not normally known for gushing about anything, reciprocated Cruise's filial affection. Pop psychologists might hypothesize that Cruise was seeking substitutes for his own absentee father.

A.E. Hotchner, Hemingway's biographer, is a close friend of Newman, and the writer couldn't resist putting a Freudian gloss on the surrogate father theory. "They are genuinely fond of each other," he said, referring to Newman and Cruise. "They had a wonderful time working together, and it's patently the cliché thing of the father and son. That really was what [enriched] the movie relationship."

Newman introduced Cruise to the world of stock car racing, which he fell in love with a decade earlier while making *Winning*, a drama about the sport. Fabulously wealthy actors occupy a different universe. When Newman invited Cruise to go for a spin in a stock car, they rented a track! The bonding was complete when they squeezed into a race car together. "Newman," Cruise recalled, "took me out and spent a lot of time talking about it. I've always loved cars and motorcycles and stuff. Racing is one thing I said that I wanted him to get me into."

Despite the forty-year age difference between the two men, Cruise, the perfectionist, couldn't resist competing with his surrogate dad, Newman. He felt compelled to go one on one with Newman at the pool table. "We used to play each other all the time. I beat him every now and then, but most of the time he beats me," Cruise remembered.

The young actor was being his typical modest self. Mike Sigel, a pool champion and advisor on the film, speculated that if Cruise ever gave up his "day job" as a movie star, he could go professional in billiards. Said Sigel, "He plays great. If he was to just continue playing, he would probably be a great player." Sigel was especially impressed with what a quick study the novice pool player was. "He shot a masse shot, which is probably the most difficult shot in pool, where you actually curve the cue ball hitting down on it. I was fooling around with the shot, and he said, 'Let me see that shot.' I explained it once, and he did it, and he made it three times in a row. Unbelievable!"

For *Top Gun* Cruise learned how to fly a jet. The technical advisor on the set of *Days of Thunder* bragged that his protégé could become a professional stock-car driver. And in *The Color of Money* he became a pool hustler. (You can almost suspect that if he ever played a brain surgeon, he'd prepare for the role by hanging out in operating rooms and begging to make "just one little incision, Sir.")

The off-screen competitiveness between Cruise an Newman was an example of life imitating art. In *The Color of Money* Cruise and Newman spend much of the time competing with each other for the unofficial crown of king of the pool hall. Their gentle off-screen competitiveness over the same sport had to have enriched their on-screen rivalry.

Cruise may have admired Newman a little too much. At least that's what the *New York Times*'s Jane Maslin felt about their on-screen relationship. Cruise was supposed to be playing a cool jerk or "flake" as he was described by the screenwriter, Richard Price.

Maslin felt Cruise's nice-guy personality undercut his character's not-so-nice-guy persona. "Mr. Cruise...seems so soft-edged and eager to please, he doesn't seem to fit the screenplay's description of Vincent as a 'natural character, an incredible flake.'"

Ironically, Cruise's off-screen kowtowing to Newman perhaps enriched the older actor's performance while diluting the nastiness of Cruise's pool shark. "Mr. Newman makes his affinity for [Cruise's character] so palpable that it creates its own promise," Maslin wrote in her review.

Another critic, David Denby of *New York* magazine, was more bullish on Cruise's interpretation and called it "the most affected acting he's done so far." But he praised Cruise's lack of vanity in allowing the director to coif him with a greaser pompadour.

Cruise's charm infected Newman, turning the sixty-one-year-old actor into a Tom Cruise fan. "He's got a lot of actor's courage," Newman boasted about his protégé. He doesn't mind climbing up there and jumping off. It's nice to watch that."

Newman described their mentor/disciple relationship with a dirty joke: "An old bull and a young bull were walking together on a ridge when they spotted a herd of cows down below. The young bull says, 'Let's run down and jump one of them cows!' The old bull says, 'Naw. Let's *walk* down the hill and jump 'em *all*!'" If only Cruise had enjoyed as healthy a relationship with his real father as he did with Paul Newman.

It's testament to Cruise's brat-free personality that he was able to charm senior stars whose reputations ranged from crusty to cranky to downright truculent.

Newman, never the most personable of stars, was charmed into gushing over his deferential disciple. "He is the prince who will inherit the crown," Newman said somewhat presumptuously, and added, "We never seriously considered anyone else" for the role. "I'd only seen *Risky Business*, but you don't have to see a lot more to know Tom is a bold, ingenious actor with a lot of courage. He's willing to try anything."

At least one person on the set was less than charmed by Cruise's habit of "sir-ing" and "ma'am-ing" everybody, from lowly grips to one of the greatest directors of all time. Scorsese admitted that he found being addressed as "sir" by the young actor a little creepy because it reminded him that he was getting on in years.

Scorsese said, "He called Newman ["sir"] also...It gets to be so ridiculous. Some of it is good because there's a lot of intensity there, and to have the politeness sometimes is a little easier. Then you can get past the politeness and get down to things. But at first, it was disconcerting. I mean I'm old but I'm not *that* old!"

After filming, Newman was still bullish on his protégé and said, "This kid has the head and balls to be one of the great ones...the next Hollywood legend."

Oliver Stone, who would later direct him in two films, after Cruise had become a legend, also felt he was Newman's heir, and threw in another matinée idol for good measure. Said Stone, "I predict a blazing, brilliant future for him. He could be another Paul Newman. He has those American good looks and a surprising agility and grace—a lot of what Redford and Newman have. I've met both of those guys, and what amazes me about them is their physical dexterity, their litheness. Tom has that too."

These encomiums are even more surprising since they come from Newman, a star who is so aloof he refuses fans' requests for autographs, and from Stone, who has publicly called Al Pacino a "schmuck." (It would be fascinating to see what Cruise could do with a real curmudgeon like Kirk Douglas or Gregory Peck, but neither actor is hot enough to land a role in a Tom Cruise film.)

However, despite their camaraderie, during the shooting of *The Color of Money* Cruise's workaholism became a bit too much for Newman—no slouch himself as the prolific star of nearly fifty films. During production of the film, Newman sent Cruise a six-pack of beer with a note that said, "Relax, kid. Drink all of it." (There's a grisly irony to Newman's note since his own son, Scott, died of a drug overdose. After the tragedy, his father funded a foundation in his son's name to combat substance abuse.)

Cruise, a teetotaller, probably distributed the beer to the crew. If Newman really felt the need to sedate his overachieving colleague, he should have sent him a safer gift like his carbohydrate-rich bottled spaghetti sauces.

Martin Scorsese's hyperartistry unfortunately didn't rub off on Cruise, who immediately returned to his middle-brow taste in film projects. He went from class to crass in selecting his next film, the universally reviled *Cocktail*.

Even if it was an aesthetic turkey, *Cocktail* is an illuminating entry in the star's filmography. For all its low-brow content, the film embodied a theme that continues to fascinate the actor and influence his script choices to this day. In film after film he has done riffs on this recurring theme: an irresponsible young man undergoes a radical personality change by discovering moral values that transcend personal ambition and monetary success.

Says Cruise, "Good scripts stick out. They're very obvious. I like films that are an emotional roller-coaster ride. My character goes through such transitions in *Cocktail*. It's hard to find roles like that. He puts himself in the most humiliating positions. And he gets the wind knocked out of his male ego. I like that. I pick films about characters the audience can identify with. You have to be able to laugh and see something of yourself in the character on the screen—or at least know someone like him."

From such wisdom comes a billion-dollar career!

In the ultimate irony, his choice of the crassly commercial *Cocktail* represents the antithesis of the film's theme. As his crassest character, *Risky Business*'s teen pimp, liked to express his philosophy on life, "What the fuck!"

As always, Cruise put his all into the film. Just as he became a pool shark to do his own stunt work for *The Color of Money*, he transformed himself into a bartender extraordinaire for *Cocktail*. Slinging drinks was one of the few day jobs he didn't hold during his short-lived period as a starving actor, so this most unpretentious of multimillionaires tended bars at various upscale yuppie watering holes in Manhattan. As part of his "research" in mixology, he learned the acrobatic trick of resting a liquor bottle on each shoulder and pouring two drinks simultaneously.

The trick was taught to him by John J.B. Bandy, who tended bar in Southern California. Bandy is even listed in the credits as "bar advisor." Bandy took his job seriously, so seriously that when another bartender, Michael "Magic Mike" Werner, claimed that *he* had taught Cruise everything he knew about pouring liquid from a bottle, Bandy filed suit in Superior Court in Glendale, California. Bandy was incensed that Magic Mike was passing himself off as Cruise's mentor on the film and, worse, offering his services to restaurateurs as the guy who taught Tom Cruise how to pour.

Bandy explained his bizarre suit by saying, "I think it's pretty dirty of someone to try to reap money off your reputation, so I felt I needed to take legal action to put a stop to it."

The lawsuit wasn't quite as frivolous as it sounded on paper. Bandy claimed that since he had become known as Cruise's professor of mixology, his income as a bartender/consultant had increased tenfold! And his claim wasn't all hot air or self-delusion; he was interviewed about the lawsuit by The *New York Times* in New Zealand, where he was on a promotional tour for a liquor distributor that was touting him as Tom Cruise's mixology muse.

The seeming inanity of this legal mumbo jumbo contains a kernel of significance. By now, Cruise had become such a public icon that anyone could launch a full-blown career simply on the basis of his association with the superstar. If Cruise ever plays a lion tamer, no doubt his circus trainer will be able to go on national (why not international) tours as the guy who taught Tom Cruise how to whip big cats into shape.

When *Cocktail* was finally released in 1988, it was universally loathed, that is, by the critics. But by this point in his career, Cruise's films were virtually "critic-proof." Even the thumbs-down sign from the Roman Emperors of movie critics, Siskel and Ebert, couldn't discourage filmgoers.

A relatively inexpensive film, except for Cruise's superstar salary, *Cocktail* went on to earn $80 million in the US alone. As a future director of his, Rob Reiner, marvelled, "Even Tom's flops make $80 million!"

Ironically, *Cocktail*'s director, Roger Donaldson, said in an interview, "When Tom and I decided to make this movie, we said, 'Well, it might not make any money, but at least it will get good reviews.'" Donaldson's crystal ball was turned upside down as *Cocktail* was embraced by fans and excoriated by critics.

Richard Corliss, the film critic for *Time*, was among the most scathing of *Cocktail* bashers. "In an ideal suburbia," Corliss wrote, "Cruise is the boy next door, most likely to succeed . . . trouble is, he knows this . . . *Cocktail* has no other reason for being other than to market the Cruise charm like a cheap celebrity perfume."

Corliss's analogy falls apart when using Cruise and "cheap" in the same sentence. His fee plus profit participation in *Cocktail* was anything but cheap, since he took home roughly $10 million.

Unfortunately, Cruise's meticulous research methods weren't copied by the director or screenwriter. One movie critic carped that the unfashionably dressed and coiffed extras who impersonated pub crawlers looked as though they had crawled out of Des Moines, not Manhattan.

Another film critic mentioned what was obvious to anyone in the audience who read the newspapers every day. *Cocktail* seemed to be in a time warp—or at least not taking place in the late '80s when AIDS and Betty Ford had made the film's two preoccupations, sex and booze, extremely touchy subjects. *Cocktail*'s attitude toward both was extremely light and frivolous. Until he finds true love with Elizabeth Shue, Cruise's bartender demonstrates an easy-going attitude toward casual sex that is downright frightening in the middle of the AIDS epidemic. Unlike more recent films, where condom wrappers are discreetly shown on the nightstand in subtle deference to safe sex, Cruise does a lot of sleeping around with little thought to the disastrous consequences of all this Don Juanism.

In an interview, Cruise was asked why his character never whipped out a condom before bedding one of his many conquests in the course of two hours. The actor had apparently already been asked this question one too many times, since he snapped back uncharacteristically for the polite star, "Because we weren't making a sex education film. We were making entertainment."

Even more embarrassing was the film's light-hearted attitude toward alcohol consumption in the era of "just say
no.".The principals in *Cocktail* knock back cocktails with the
same guiltlessness that characters in the pre-Alcoholics Anonymous era did in frothy thirties comedies. What we would consider full-blown alcoholism today was used as an amusing plot
device then. Or as the *Los Angeles Times* noted, Nick Charles
was so drunk in all those *Thin Man* films he was probably legally unfit to drive during most of his sleuthing.

Again, all Cruise could say in defense of the film's politically incorrect attitude toward excessive drinking was that he
wasn't making a training film for AA.

*Cocktail*'s theme attracted Cruise, who told this writer that
he looks for scripts where his character is "totally different on
page 120 from where he was on page one." And by this point in
his career, if something attracted him, he got it, whether it was a
car or a movie no one else could get off the ground.

But Cruise didn't let his bankability and clout go to his
head. He was no egomaniacal Brat Packer. When I asked him if
his name alone attached to a project could get the project
bankrolled, he actually paused as though the thought had never
occurred to him.

Measuring his words, afraid to sound cocky rather than
realistic, which he was, Cruise finally said sheepishly, "At this
point, yes, I think so... "

But it took more than bankability to get *Cocktail* on
screen. The movie really got made because of Cruise's astound-
ing work ethic. Before *Cocktail,* he had already signed to make
*Rainman,* but the problem-plagued script for that film caused a
delay in the start date of principal photography.

Tom Cruise found himself with a few months free time on
his hands. Instead of luxuriating on a beach in the Caribbean,
he squeezed out enough time to learn how to bartend and make
a two-hour movie.

*Time* magazine was unimpressed by his dedication to such

an unworthy project and dismissed *Cocktail* as a "vacation from responsibility," one of the kinder brickbats hurled at the film. In his typical self-deprecating manner, Cruise himself later admitted that it was not a "crowning jewel." But that admission was made much later—after he had added several prestigious film credits to his resumé.

Any aesthetic guilt he may have felt about *Cocktail* was completely absolved by his next effort, the multiple-Oscar-winning *Rainman*.

The theme of *Rainman* was almost identical to *Cocktail*'s, but about a hundred IQ points higher. Cruise once again plays a callow young man who learns life lessons from an older mentor, in this case his autistic brother, played by Dustin Hoffman.

*Rainman* was a difficult project that Tom Cruise helped make easy. The film had resisted the rewrite efforts of Steven Spielberg, who abandoned the project. Warren Beatty, tinkerer supreme, also reportedly ran screaming from his word processor. The biggest stumbling block was how to make an interesting movie about two guys basically yelling at each other in a Porsche. *Rainman* had the distinction of being the only film that seemed claustrophobic even though it was set largely in a convertible on the open road!

The film looked as though it would remain in development purgatory until Cruise signed on. Faster than a studio chief could shout "greenlight," the project was an immediate go.

This new project came complete with a new potential father surrogate, Cruise's co-star, Dustin Hoffman. Cruise did a Newman-number on this older actor, who never met an artistic fight he didn't like. Tom's wooing of Hoffman took considerably more fortitude on the younger man's part because Hoffman, for all his talent, is infamous for being difficult. (During the editing of one of his biggest hits, *Tootsie*, Hoffman got into a now-famous screaming match with director Sydney Pollack in the Columbia parking lot in full view of amused studio employees. And defrocked film mogul David Puttnam, the classy producer of *Chariots of Fire* and *Midnight Express*, badmouthed Hoffman in so many published interviews that Hoffman eventually confronted him in a tony West Hollywood restaurant.)

As much as Newman and Cruise bonded on *The Color of Money*, working with Hoffman must have been particularly gratifying for the young star. Hoffman had always been Cruise's favorite actor. Years earlier, when Cruise was just another struggling actor/waiter, he and pals Sean Penn and Timothy Hutton found out where Hoffman lived and showed up on the star's doorstep. Of course, Cruise and his buddies were hardly stalkers, more like worshipers at the shrine of St. Dustin, but they did turn into Peeping Toms when they had the temerity to peek in windows of Hoffman's estate. However, they didn't have the nerve to knock on their culture hero's door, even though they dared one another to do so.

Only a few years later, Cruise became a major movie star with the release of *Risky Business*. By then, he didn't have to sneak onto the grounds of Hoffman's estate. Cruise was ushered into the older actor's dressing room in the Broadway theater where he was playing Willie Loman in *Death of a Salesman*.

During the filming of *Rainman*, Hoffman called Cruise a "demon," and he meant it as the ultimate compliment, made by one workaholic to another. "I don't usually meet people with my work habits," Hoffman said admiringly. "But Tom and I both like to get up before dawn and exercise. At night, Tom was constantly knocking at my door. He'd say, 'Why don't we do it this way?' And he'd do my lines so well he could have played *my* part."

And the imperious Hoffman, who sued not one but two movie studios in the '70s when his artistic input was ignored, became almost deferential to Cruise. "I started out being his mentor," Hoffman said. "But by the end, Tom was as much directing me as I was directing him. Tom's a moment to moment actor. He's there 'in the moment.' He doesn't have an intellectual idea of what he wants to do. He's coming off his

gut, and that makes him a pleasure to play ping pong with
… He's a Christmas tree, lit from head to toe."

Ironically, Hoffman, considering his years of experience,
didn't seem to have as profound an effect on his co-star as
Cruise had on Hoffman. When I asked Cruise what life lessons
he had learned from two wise old actors like Hoffman and Paul
Newman, his answer made it sound as though his greatest lesson was how to be an efficiency expert.

He replied to my question, saying, "I learned to be real
organized from both of them. They taught me how not to waste
time. For *Cocktail*, I interviewed thirty-five bartenders in two
days."

No tips on acting? No pearls of wisdom on coping with
early success? Not even pointers on how to fend off groupies?

No.

According to Cruise, two of our greatest living actors
taught him how to debrief bartenders with rapid efficiency.

Cruise, on the other hand, left a big impression on the rest
of the cast. In fact, it almost sounds as if his leading lady, Valeria
Golino, fell a little bit in love with her leading man, although
there were never any rumors about an on-set romance. Cruise
was, after all, still dating Mimi and would never be unfaithful.
(In fact, he is such a gentleman, one journalist noted approvingly that Cruise had never been accused of sexual harassment on
the set, a claim that couldn't be made for many other handsome
stars.)

In her mellifluous Italian accent, Valeria Golino described
her perfect co-star to *People* magazine, "He's protective and
strong and still innocent. His most attractive feature is his eyes.
Not their color. His 'regard.' The way he looks with them.
They're very alive."

Even the film's producer, Mark Johnson, paid Cruise a
back-handed compliment about his looks. "His smile is a little
off. The nose is a little off. But it's the sum total."

After the film was released in 1988, Cruise's instinct that *Rainman* was a worthwhile project paid off for just about everyone but himself at Oscar time.

*Rainman* swept the Oscars, winning Hoffman a best actor award and Barry Levinson his first best director award along with best picture and best original screenplay. Cruise was shut out. The Academy didn't even deign to nominate him.

But Cruise earned his biggest paycheck to that date, $3 million, for the film. And a project which several studios had turned down as uncommercial ended up grossing $173 million domestically. His ability to pick a winner that every other power in the industry thought was a loser gave him instant credibility as a guy with a golden gut. Film executives have made entire careers on the strength of picking one big hit even if all their previous and following efforts are failures.

In a witty acceptance speech at the Oscars, genial director Barry Levinson acknowledged Cruise's enormous contribution to the film, including getting the dead project off the ground. Levinson later speculated on why Cruise was in danger of becoming the Rodney Dangerfield of superstars, a guy who couldn't get any respect.

*Time* magazine said Cruise wasn't "as pretty as Rob Lowe." But Levinson actually felt Cruise's "prettiness" got in the way of the respect he deserved as an actor. "Tom is at a disadvantage," Levinson said in a *Time* cover story on Cruise. "He's got such a pretty face his abilities are underestimated. And he's not working a rebel image, which is associated with being a good actor."

# TEN

# Born Under a Lucky Star

U niversal didn't want to touch a Vietnam protest movie about a creepy cripple with a ten-foot catheter. Ron Kovic, the Vietnam vet who had written the book on which the script was based, had spent ten years in Hollywood trying to get his uncommercial life story on the big screen. Even when Oscar-winning director Oliver Stone expressed interest in the project, Universal still balked. As in the case with *Rainman*, once the billion-dollar man expressed interest, however, the studio gave him *carte blanche*.

After ten years of bashing his head against the wall of Hollywood indifference, Kovic could only compare his good fortune to another screen hero who had divine intercession on his side. "I feel like Jimmy Stewart in *It's a Wonderful Life!*" Kovic said. In the Capra classic, an angel from heaven performed miracles to help a suicidal Jimmy Stewart. As far as Kovic was concerned, Tom Cruise was his angel, the man with the near divine power to get any project off the ground.

Once Cruise expressed interest, Universal was ready to give him *carte blanche* but not a blank check. Under the Scrooge-like control of studio chief Sid Sheinberg, Universal has made cost-containment during his twenty-year tenure a personal fetish.

Cruise was welcomed to Steven Spielberg's home studio with open arms—and closed checkbook.

Cruise could make his "baby," but he'd have to do it for scale. After pocketing $3 million for *Rainman*, Cruise could have topped that figure at any studio in town if he was willing to do a riff on *Top Gun* or *Cocktail*. The multimillionaire actor may be the least greedy star in Hollywood. He worked for scale on a project he loved, *Born on the Fourth of July*, when he could have made $10 million on a project the studios loved. His indifference to money almost makes you suspect he'd work for free if that was the only way to get a script he loved into production.

"If I want to do something, money is never an issue," said Cruise, whose childhood was dominated by the issue of money, or lack thereof. "I've never thought when becoming an actor of making a lot of money. I'd always thought of making good movies."

Nevertheless, Cruise would agree with Sophie Tucker's famous epigram: "I've been rich, and I've been poor... Rich is better."

Or in Cruise's words, money is "nice, because I didn't grow up with money, and to be able to do things for my family is nice." The almighty dollar, he added, is "just icing on the cake. The important thing is the artistic freedom."

Not surprisingly, the exceedingly unpalatable *Born on the Fourth of July* script had been hobbling from studio to studio for eleven years. After reading only the first twenty pages, however, Cruise called his longtime agent, Paula Wagner, who now heads his production company at Paramount, and said, "I don't care what it takes. I want to make this movie." What it took was a lot of humble-pie eating on Cruise's part.

Amazingly, Cruise, one of the savviest money manager/ stars, agreed to the insulting offer of scale, which was $50,000 at the time. His acquiescence wasn't quite as generous—or crazy—as it sounded. But it did show that he was still a gambler. If *Born on the Fourth of July* flopped, Cruise would get

$50,000 and nothing more. But because of his profit participation in the film, if it hit big, so would his bank account. His *Cocktail* director, Roger Donaldson, explained Cruise's attitude toward film art and the bottom line. "Tom doesn't go into a movie thinking, 'God, this is going to make me rich!'" (Of course, Cruise doesn't have to since he's already joined the ranks of the super-rich.)

In *Born on the Fourth of July*, Tom Cruise would urinate and defecate on himself and scream "penis" repeatedly at his screen mother. The Academy loves this sort of self-defilement and finally awarded him an Oscar nomination for his turn as a paraplegic. (Interestingly, Daniel Day-Lewis would win the Oscar that year for out-handicapping Cruise as a quadraplegic in *My Left Foot*. In a typical burst of modesty and generosity, Cruise let out a cheer at the Oscars when Day-Lewis's name was announced as the best actor winner.)

Unlike the Academy of Arts & Sciences, the art-house film critic Stanley Kaufman of the august (and little read) *New Republic* was not impressed with Cruise's masochistic stretching in a wheelchair. Kaufman wrote that "his voice is too thin and high pitched," a strange complaint since the real-life character Cruise played, Ron Kovic, is whiney voiced enough to have guest-starred on *thirtysomething*.

Prior to the film's release, a cheeky British magazine said, "The thought of Tom Cruise in a wheelchair is as terrifying as Sean Penn starring in *Gandhi II*."

Worse has been written about Cruise.

A reporter once had the temerity to read Pauline Kael's review of *Rainman* to Cruise during an interview. Kael, the Torquemada of film criticism, wrote, "Cruise as a slimeball is just a sugarpuss in Italian tailoring...He's an actor in the same sense that Robert Taylor was an actor. He's patented; his knowing that a camera is on him produces nothing but fraudulence."

Cruise mercifully had not seen the Kael review until the reporter handed him a copy of it. The interviewer was mortified when he immediately realized that because of Cruise's dyslexia he couldn't skim through the review. Ever helpful, the reporter read choice bits of venom from Kael's diatribe.

The superstar's reaction is telling. After a long silence, Cruise simply replied, "It's her opinion, and she's entitled to it."

Much later and more defensively, he would say of Cruise-hating critics, "There are critics who don't like movies, actors. It's amazing. Those people tend to spread their disease, attempt to spread it. For me, it's not just about getting good reviews, but about reading something smart."

Armani-suitless, Cruise would show Kael and the world that he was no Robert Taylor. *Born on the Fourth of July* not only demonstrated that Cruise was the least vain actor in Hollywood, but one of the least greedy as well.

Some felt that Cruise's decision to take on such an iffy project showed he was crazy like a fox. Others thought it more accurate to say crazy like a financier.

Once Cruise signed on to the project, his usual workaholism took over. This time, however, his method acting approached madness. It was a madness encouraged by director Stone, something of a mad genius himself.

Ron Kovic, a Vietnam vet turned Vietnam War protester, had been wounded in combat, his spine shattered, leaving him unable to walk. Just as he had spent seven weeks hanging around a pool table for those laws-of-physics-defying bank shots in *The Color of Money*, Cruise parked his butt in a wheelchair, refusing to get up for days at a time.

That's vintage method acting preparation. But what he was willing to do beyond that smacks of lunacy—or an extreme need to fully immerse himself in a character's way of life. Oliver Stone suggested the crazy idea, and Cruise enthusiastically agreed. Stone wanted to inject a serum into Cruise's billion-dollar behind that would totally paralyze the actor for forty-eight hours! That sounds like overkill, since Kovic was only paralyzed from the waist down. The situation was even more perilous. As Stone casually mentioned, there was a "slight" possibility that the serum could permanently paralyze the superstar. That caveat didn't scare off either men. Cruise wanted to feel the impotence and rage of being totally immobile.

The experiment no doubt would have taken place. Nobody says no to a man who can enrich a studio by $400 million a picture—nobody except the completion bond company which had insured the cast. The company was not willing to take the chance that the star might collect lost wages—for life—if the serum turned him into a vegetable. Cruise's films had already earned close to a billion dollars, and the idea of calculating what his lifelong lost wages would total must have given insurance underwriters nightsweats.

Stone, something of an obsessive himself, was happy to feed into Cruise's fetish for research. The director sent him to boot camp not once but twice. The normally pampered superstar submitted to the regimen without a whimper.

Stone, who has been known to badmouth actors (he called Al Pacino a schmuck when the actor backed out of *Born on the Fourth of July* years earlier), repaid Cruise's pliant behavior with a peculiar compliment. The director told his star, "You have a Homeric personality, and you are aware of your star destiny." Stone later suggested an alternate source of Cruise's enduring popularity when he said, "He's a kid off a Wheaties box!"

Sometimes the actor could be too convincing in a role. Kovic was on the set most of the time as technical advisor; he also wrote a pivotal scene without any input from Stone at the director's request and eventually shared a screenwriting credit with Stone. In the movie, Cruise comes home drunk one night and screams at his mother, "There is no God. There is no country, just me in the wheelchair for the rest of my life."

Kovic later admitted that Cruise's performance in that scene was so achingly true to the real incident from his life,

Kovic had to leave the set. "I just couldn't take it," he said.

As Kovic was driving himself to his hotel after fleeing the set, a Jeep pulled up next to him. Cruise was behind the wheel and rolled down his window. "Why does your life have to be so difficult?" he joked. Kovic was not amused and screamed obscenities at the superstar.

Cruise's method acting also took less pathological forms. To stay in character while shooting, method prima donnas like Meryl Streep hold on to their accents even when the camera isn't rolling. Reporters who interviewed Streep on the set of *Sophie's Choice* had to talk to a woman with an almost impenetrable Polish accent—Streep in character.

Typically, Cruise even took his methodical ways off the set. For an interview with *Vanity Fair* during filming of *Born on the Fourth of July*, reporter Jesse Kornbluth thought he had been stood up by the star when he didn't appear at a restaurant as scheduled.

Cruise is too polite to do anything of the sort. He did show up, but in character as Ron Kovic, complete with (shaved) receding hairline, a week's worth of beard and a baseball cap. And he rolled into the restaurant in a wheelchair!

The reporter didn't recognize him, and neither did any of the diners. For once during an interview in a public place, Cruise would not be repeatedly interrupted by autograph hounds.

For his role as a high school football star in *All the Right Moves*, Cruise went incognito to football practice at a high school in New Jersey. For *Born on the Fourth of July*, he chose a grimmer method of research, visiting VA hospitals. For more authenticity, an expert on rehabilitation was hired and reported to the set every day, watching for any Hollywood-type softening of the grimness of life in a rehab hospital.

One disabled vet, Matt Raible, who attended a special screening, vouched for the authenticity of the film and insisted that for once Hollywood had gotten it right. One of the more unwatchable scenes in the film depicted urine and fecal drainage bags overflowing on to the floor, while rats scampered in the mess. Raible confirmed that the real-life VA hospitals were every bit as grim as Hollywood's recreation of it.

The experience at the VA hospitals saddened Cruise at the same time that it made him realize what a great life he had, even without the superstar perks and paydays. At one hospital, he recalled, "I talked to a guy who'd wrecked his motorcycle, a kid who was shot in a parking lot, a child who was just playing in the ocean and is now paralyzed for life. I saw their different stages of denial."

His wheelchair-bound "research" made him play paraplegic make believe. "I spent a lot of time in a wheelchair also, even before shooting," he said.

Cruise rolled out on the town, visiting a skating rink and an electronics store. Rinkside, he spotted a youth who was also in a wheelchair. Cruise, unrecognizable with his grunge look and shaved head, rolled right over to the kid and said, "Hey, man, what's your name? Some shopping center, huh? Where are you from?"

The two talked about the Olympics and a restaurant where the boy had eaten lunch. Finally, Cruise said to him, "Well, you take care of yourself," patted the boy's arm and rolled off.

The trip to the electronics store wasn't so touchy-feely. Maybe he was just staying in character and displaying some of Kovic's documented rage at a world that is not always "handicap friendly."

Cruise and Kovic often went shopping in matching wheelchairs. In a Westwood, California, electronics store near UCLA, a salesperson asked the two men to leave because their wheels were leaving marks on the rubber carpet. Kovic remembered the embarrassing incident with pride. "Tom was furious. Everyone in the store turned and looked at him when he shouted, 'I have as much right to be in this store as everyone else!'"

Kovic totally bonded with the man who was playing him on screen. The two men shared similar working-class backgrounds, although after high school Kovic went off to the nightmare that was Vietnam, and Cruise went to New York to become a star. Both men were raised Catholic and were stars of the high school wrestling team. The first time they met at Kovic's home, the effusive star trotted up the driveway and hugged him.

Sean Penn and Charlie Sheen had been in the running for the role, and Kovic was worried that Cruise's "cool jerk" persona would turn his life's story into something like *Top Gun Goes to Vietnam and Gets Crippled*. The hug changed his mind immediately. "I had my doubts before he came over that day. I wondered if he had the depth to portray me."

On Cruise's birthday, the vet gave him his Bronze Star. "He came up to me on my birthday, gave me a hug, and said he was so proud and that he loved me," Cruise said.

Cruise told Kovic he wanted him to see the completed film and feel it was accurate and true to the spirit of Kovic's autobiography. After a screening, Kovic said simply, "That's the way it was."

*Born on the Fourth of July*—the "uncommercial" film, produced for less than $20 million (that's pocket change for Schwarzenegger or Stallone)—raked in $70 million in the US alone. *Parade* magazine reported that Cruise's big gamble paid off like a Vegas slot machine, turning the star's meager fifty grand into $7 million from his profit participation deal.

However, not everyone was pleased with the film. Cruise's method acting was too convincing for one disabled person, Lake Nofer, who wrote an angry letter to the editor that ran in the *Los Angeles Times*. While praising Daniel Day-Lewis's turn as a quadriplegic in *My Left Foot*, the letter writer, bound to a wheelchair due to multiple sclerosis, blasted Cruise for making his portrayal of a paraplegic so creepy. "People often assume my life is more dismal than it really is," Nofer wrote. "*Born on the Fourth of July* reinforces that notion. By contrast, when I saw *My Left Foot*, I felt I could do anything."

So Cruise wouldn't win any popularity awards from organizations for the disabled. And he eventually lost the Oscar to Day-Lewis. But as the balding paraplegic he had pleased himself and shown that he didn't have to rely on a killer bod and grin to make a critically and commercially successful film.

*The New York Time's* venerable Vincent Canby commented on Cruise's good looks then paid him the highest compliment by noting that the actor didn't use them to soften an often prickly characterization. "Though ideally handsome, Mr. Cruise looks absolutely right... Watching the evolution of his Ron Kovic... is both harrowing and inspiring."

*New York* magazine said approvingly, "Cruise has dropped his confident smile. In the past, he has seemed callow, a failing he disguised with cockiness. He gives a brave and vulnerable performance."

*Newsweek* fell all over itself praising Cruise's stretch in *Born on the Fourth of July.* "It's up to Cruise to carry the film, and he traces Kovic's transition from naive jock to agonized survivor with fierce conviction. There's a blunt power in Cruise we haven't seen before."

Even the *New Yorker's* gangsterish Pauline Kael forced herself to praise Cruise while panning—as usual—the rest of the movie: "He disappears inside Ron Kovic's receding hairline, Fu Manchu mustache, and long, matted hair."

The most rewarding notices, however, came from Kovic himself, who said simply, "I truly believe Tom became *me*." That's high praise indeed from a man who originally feared the actor would soft-pedal the role into unrecognizability.

*Born on the Fourth of July* affected audiences to such an extent that the Democratic Congressional Campaign Committee, which funds Democratic candidates in crucial races, begged Kovic to run for Congress against ultraright-wing Congressman Robert K. Dornan, infamous for his attacks on homosexuals and pro-abortion activists. Kovic had never held office before, but the power of the film so mesmerized these sophisticated politicoes, that they were willing to put the resources of the Democratic Party at Kovic's feet. It would have been a sweet irony for Kovic to run against the right-wing Dornan, since Kovic had himself been a died-in-the-wool-conservative until Vietnam transformed him into a left-wing idealogue.

Ultimately Kovic decided not to tilt at windmills since Dornan represented an ultraconservative constituency in Orange County, California, where Kovic's liberalism would have been anathema. But the fact that he was wooed by the Democratic party reinforces the power of Hollywood's screen iconography.

According to the director, the film also had a life-changing effect on the actor and his lightweight image. "I think Tom became middle aged making this movie. I think he passed out of his youth truly into early middle age. He'll never be the same boy that he was before. He knows too much now."

Stone's assessment turned out to be dead wrong. Cruise's next two films would suggest he was a still a boy, but he was a boy with enough clout to get any project he wanted off the ground.

# ELEVEN

# A Few Good Flops

**B**lame it on Paul Newman. The professional actor and salad dressing manufacturer is also an amateur race-car driver. During filming of *The Color of Money*, Newman infected his co-star with the same bug that had bitten him two decades earlier.

Newman would make a flop about the racing world called *Winning* to stoke his speed fever. Cruise would also make a flop, his first in years, to gratify his need for speed.

*Days of Thunder* had an A-list pedigree—and a curse.

The original screenwriter, Warren Skaaren, who had co-written *Top Gun* and *Batman*, couldn't get a handle on the story. Not even after seven drafts.

Robert Towne, who has written what is considered one of the greatest screenplays ever filmed, *Chinatown*, was called in to do liposuction on the bloated script.

The script, all seven incarnations of it, was a mess. And Towne had the clout and track record to throw out every one of Skaaren's drafts and start from scratch.

Even more than for *Chinatown*, which is after all a twenty-year-old movie, Towne is famous in Hollywood as a script doctor, one who can operate quickly and efficiently under a tight deadline. He performed life-saving surgery on *Bonnie and Clyde*, *The Godfather*, and other films, all uncredited.

The film was already in production, and chaos ensued as Towne literally pulled pages out of his typewriter and handed them to Cruise and the rest of the cast just before filming the scene.

Cruise wore earphones in the racecar, standard equipment for all drivers. But they were more than a prop for the actor. They were a lifeline. During one racing scene, Towne actually read Cruise's lines to him over the headphones as the cameras were rolling.

The need for such drastic rewrites may have come from the story's provenance. The Oscar-winning writer was working from "an original story by Tom Cruise," according to the film's final credits.

Four years before he made *Days of Thunder*, Cruise went for a spin with Newman on the track of the Daytona International Speedway, which hosts the Daytona 500, the Wimbledon of the hot-rod set. Cruise schmoozed with the drivers and pit crews, then he got into the driver's seat of a stock car. As he pushed the accelerator to the floor, the young actor practically had an agnostic religious experience. His vision improved. Whenever he blinked, another hundred yards went by. When the car made a sharp turn, the force of gravity made his head feel as though it weighed a ton.

All that doesn't sound like a particularly pleasant experience, but for Cruise, it was near orgasmic. Cruise owned a Porsche, which he had drag raced before. But the Daytona track was the Oscars of racing. And he wanted to win one. As soon as he got out of the car, he said to himself, "I'm going to make a movie about this."

Cruise sat down at a typewriter and banged out a brief outline. A film buff, if not a film scholar, the actor realized he was treading on slippery territory. Hollywood had never made a successful film about the world of stock car racing. Newman's own effort, *Winning*, is a credit the actor would probably like to delete from his bio. The great Al Pacino hit the skids with

*Bobby Deerfield. Grand Prix* was an expensive embarrassment starring James Garner. If there's a stronger term for embarrassment, it should be applied to Kenny Rogers's *Six Pack*, which miscast the chubby country western singer as a cool racecar driver. *Speedway*, on the other hand, was just one of Elvis Presley's many laughable excursions on film.

Cruise knew about the racecar curse in movies, and he knew why they had all laid an egg. "I'd never seen a racecar picture done well," Cruise said while shooting his racecar picture. "A lot of them didn't have a story, just the action. As a result, you felt separated from the movie. I mean, I don't care how much machinery you have in a film. If I can't get involved with the characters, then for my money I'm not going to enjoy it. I want the racing scenes to punctuate what's happening in the characters' lives."

This savvy analysis suggests the real reason for Cruise's monumental success. He would make a fine movie studio executive if he weren't already gainfully employed as a movie star. His real talent lies not in his winning smile, gorgeous face, buffed bod, or even his infamous perfectionism.

The real reason Cruise has stayed on top of the box-office hill for more than a decade is a simple one. The reason is simple, but the execution is not. Cruise can read a script and nine times out of ten predict whether or not it will be a commercial success.

That's a talent every development executive in the film industry would sacrifice his first-born child for—or even more significantly, his corner table at Morton's. If any Tom, Dick, or Sherry Lansing could read a script and gauge its box-office performance, Hollywood would only bankroll blockbusters. But film is such a visual medium, it's almost impossible to look at the word on a page and visualize it on screen.

Even respected actors like Meryl Streep and Robert De Niro don't have this knack for separating the dross from the golden script.

Cruise is no De Niro, but then De Niro is no Cruise when it comes to divining what will be a hit and what will be *Howard the Duck*.

This extraordinary talent has allowed Cruise to treat screenwriters with a certain disdain which is alien to the way he treats most people. An incident on the set showed that while Cruise was deferential to idols like Dustin Hoffman and Paul Newman, he considered the writer, no matter how respected in his field, part of the support staff. After all, the story was Cruise's idea, not Towne's. With no sense that he was arguing with the Hemingway of screenwriters, Cruise told Towne to delete a crucial speech in the film. It's testament to Cruise's putting the project above everything else, even his new lady love, that the speech he wanted axed was supposed to be delivered by Kidman.

And the reason he wanted her speech killed had to do with his growing obsession over control. Not his, Tom Cruise's control, but the control exerted in the film by the *character* he plays.

The speech by Kidman, written by Towne, represents the antithesis of what Cruise believes in.

After Cruise's friend dies in a racing accident in the story, Kidman's neurologist gives him a lecture that's supposed to offer consolation.

It gave him heartburn instead.

Cruise's character is blaming himself for his friend's death, even though it was an accident, and the character had nothing to do with it. Kidman tells him that control is an illusion, and only "infantile egomaniacs don't know that."

Them's fightin' words to a man who forged a successful career by exerting just such total control over every aspect of it. He certainly didn't like his life philosophy being attributed to "infantile egomania," even if it was his character, not him, being so labeled.

Cruise had the temerity to tell Towne that Kidman's speech was bullshit because the actor had demonstrated quite effectively that the individual *can* control things. (Up to the then, the only film he hadn't been able to control to blockbuster status was *Legend*.)

Cruise may be a control freak, but he's not a tyrant. Towne convinced Cruise that the scene was crucial to transform his character's value system. In fact, Towne noted that Cruise's real-life reaction was exactly what the character's should be.

Cruise caved. The speech stayed.

If only Cruise had caved in on the whole concept, which he supplied, and let Towne write him a really good script based on an idea from Towne, maybe he could've had a chance at success.

For *Chinatown*, Towne used the stylish film noir detective mysteries of the '30s and '40s as his model. Unfortunately, for *Days of Thunder* he was forced to use an idea that had come out of Cruise's feverish brain.

A movie star with clout can be a scary thing. After an actor or actress enjoys a huge commercial success, the white-hot star supernovas and becomes bankable. That means the actor can get just about any project off the ground. And when a star whose only talent is acting decides he or she is a filmmaker, it's more often than not a recipe for disaster.

After grossing more than the GNP of several Latin American countries with his two *Die Hard* flicks, Bruce Willis was so hot he could have chosen for his next project an all-singing, all-dancing revue based on the *Tibetan Book of the Dead*. Instead, he chose a project almost as noxious, *Hudson Hawk*.

Bruce became an *auteur*. He not only came up with the story line, based on his experience with a wind that whips through Manhattan called the Hudson Hawk, but during filming he meddled in directing and frequently overruled the director. The result has become a touchstone for comedians when they want a quick reference for the quintessential flop, replacing *Heaven's Gate* and *Howard the Duck* as Hollywood's most embarrassing turkeys.

The list of stars who think their box-office success has earned them the mantle of *auteur* is long and full of embarrassments: Goldie Hawn imperiously recutting *Swing Shift* to refocus it from a feminist buddy film to a romantic melodrama flick emphasizing the role of her new boyfriend, Kurt Russell. Or Sylvester Stallone, creating rancid cookie cutter versions of *Rocky* and *Rambo*, like *Over the Top* and *Cobra*.

But stars who suddenly think they're Scorsese after doing boffo box office aren't always an unmitigated disaster. *Man Without a Face* didn't do *Lethal Weapon* business, but it was respectfully received.

And then there are the big exceptions to this nightmare of every studio chief and stockholder. Stars who do indeed become *auteurs*. The prerelease word of mouth about Kevin Costner's *Dances With Wolves*, if anyone remembers after its Oscar sweep, said it was a masturbatory fantasy Orion let Costner indulge in, hoping to retain his services for something a bit more mainstream and commercial at the studio. At the time, Westerns were as dead as Chevy Chase's talk show career.

Clint Eastwood had been considered a journeyman director and a fading box-office draw until *Unforgiven* put him in the same league as John Ford and Sam Peckinpah.

And even Whoopi Goldberg earned the respect of Disney executives after *Sister Act* became a hit. During filming, however, Disney gave her so much grief when she demanded changes in the script the actress showed up on the set wearing Mickey Mouse ears and a T-shirt that said, "Nigger-teer." Annette Funicello would have wept. The commercial success of *Sister Act* gave her so much credibility with the Mickey Mouse executives that they gave her total control over the sequel, which flopped.

Executives at Paramount were doing anything *but* weeping

when Cruise came to them with the concept for *Days of Thunder*. Next to sequels, the thing that most gladdens the hearts of the studio suits is a clone of a previous blockbuster.

If Cruise had had to go through the humiliation of pitching the story to Paramount executives, which he didn't, *Days of Thunder* might have been described as *Top Gun Goes to the Races*.

It was a trip Paramount was more than happy to make. So what if the film's projected $50-million budget ended up pulling $70 million into the black hole that superstar vehicles often become?

*Top Gun* had already grossed close to half a billion dollars worldwide, making Cruise's box-office pull greater than Luke Skywalker's or Captain Kirk's. If Cruise could work the same money magic on *Days of Thunder*, and he already had with much less commercial projects like *Born on the Fourth of July* and *Rainman*, who cared if the film cost $70 million, a piddling amount compared to a possible half-billion-dollar payoff?

Cruise has always been a gambler when it comes to picking projects. Studio execs, answerable to stockholders, are less willing to gamble. But *Days of Thunder* seemed like a sure thing.

William Goldman, the Oscar-winning screenwriter of *Butch Cassidy and the Sundance Kid* and *Maverick*, once wrote that in Hollywood "nobody knows anything." Goldman, a professional gadfly as well as author, never met Cruise, because if he had, he would have amended his rule to "Tom Cruise knows everything *most* of the time."

Unfortunately, this time Cruise's "golden gut" deserted him, and the film itself did nothing for Cruise's career.

*Days of Thunder* grossed $40 million in its opening weekend on the Fourth of July, 1990, and Paramount executives felt sure they had another *Top Gun* on their hands and balance sheets. Alas, *Days of Thunder* hit a brick wall after word of mouth got out (helped along by unkind reviews) that the film was only a pallid copy of *Top Gun*. As the unfortunate people who paid $7.50 to see this uninspired clone already know, Cruise played a NASCAR driver obsessed with winning at any cost. When a friend suffers brain damage and dies, Cruise as he had in *Top Gun*, undergoes an almost religious conversion and discovers there are more important things than win, win, win. (That plot twist doesn't sound autobiographical at all, since Cruise is still grabbing at the brass ring. Maybe the on-screen conversion represents a value system he would like to undergo—at a much later date, perhaps when he's ready to collect Social Security and the only work available is on TV.)

One critic called the story line "road kill," and others carped that the supposedly realistic film exaggerated the amount of "bumping and rubbing" that takes place during a race. Afficionados of the sport noted that the film made stock-car racing look like a bumper-car ride at an amusement park. Cruise likes to compare his action films to an "E-ticket ride" at Disneyland, in other words, the best and most expensive of all rides at the park. Detractors complained that the film had all the excitement and scope of a bumper car going three miles per hour.

*Days of Thunder* was no *Top Gun*. And that was fine with Cruise, although he may have wished their box-office takes were more similar. The actor especially objected to thematic comparisons of the two films, even though both their themes featured a brash young man learning human values. Only the hardware, one critic quipped, was different.

The actor hates being accused of copying himself or capitalizing on past successes by rehashing old movies in new settings. Although his characters of Cole Trickle in *Days of Thunder* and Maverick in *Top Gun* could be almost the same person, Cruise adamantly denies the two are screen clones of one another. "Cole and Maverick are different people going through things differently," he has said. He insists, with some justification, that there is no such thing as the "typical" Tom

Cruise role, since he's played everything from a paraplegic in a wheelchair to a teen pimp in a Porsche.

For once in his life, Cruise didn't care about failing when *Days of Thunder* hit the skids at the box office. The film grossed $82 million, but its bloated budget of $70 million meant it failed to turn a profit when marketing costs were factored in.

He could console himself with his upfront salary of $9 million, which was not tied to profit participation in the film, a lucky break since there is no profit participation on a film that doesn't turn a profit!

But an even bigger consolation was meeting Kidman, who at twenty-two was hilariously miscast (by Cruise) as a neurologist/brain surgeon. Kidman defended her co-star's casting decision. There are glamorous female physicians who look like movie stars, although she didn't try to stretch that contention by adding there were brain surgeons as young as she was at the time. "I've been to women doctors who were incredibly good looking. It's not legitimate to criticize me for being too stylish in *Days of Thunder*. I didn't try to pull my hair back and wear glasses and look goofy because that's the stereotype of the doctor."

Cruise didn't care if Kidman was all wrong for the part. She was all right for him. He had seen her in a low-budget Australian thriller, *Dead Calm*, a Hitchcock-like gem in which she single-handedly defeated a serial murderer on a becalmed yacht in the middle of the Pacific.

Cruise wanted Kidman. Paramount, the happy home of the half-billion dollar *Top Gun*, wanted whatever Tom wanted. If he had asked to make an R-rated film with Jessica Tandy as the object of his lust, the studio would have said yes. Kidman as a brain surgeon who looked like a Roman Polanski date was almost as preposterous, but Paramount was happy to oblige, hoping this *Top Gun* clone would bring in perhaps another half a billion.

What Cruise lacked in aesthetic judgment, he once again

made up for with workaholism and perfectionism. He had never driven a stock car before, but after a crash course in the sport, he stunned professionals at the track in North Carolina by turning laps at 182 miles per hour. Bob Bondurant, the technical advisor on the film, claimed that Cruise could turn pro if he ever gave up acting.

As he would masochistically do in the boxing scenes of his next film, Cruise did all but a handful of the driving scenes.

Racing officials were so starstruck, they even allowed Paramount to put two movie stunt cars in the real thing, the Daytona 500, the Super Bowl of stock-car racing, although these bogus prop cars did only forty laps.

Like too many other method actors, Cruise's method of researching his role approached if not madness, at least a scary disregard for life—his own.

While studying at Bob Bondurant's School of High Performance Driving near San Francisco, Bondurant recalls with horror Cruise's daredevil driving. The memory is also tinged with amazement over the actor's casual disregard for life, limb, and property, plus gratitude for the alacrity with which he paid for all the mayhem the superstar caused on the track. "Tom drove like he was out of his mind. He crashed up three cars, split one right down the middle. Each time he would pull out his checkbook and pay for the car. I think he spent something like $100,000 that way," Bondurant marveled.

Problems arose when Cruise took his "need for speed" off track. During a break in shooting, the police picked him up for driving sixty-six miles per hour in a thirty-five-miles-per-hour zone in Darlington, North Carolina.

Cruise got off lightly with a $125 fine. He should have paid more, but the judge, like just about every other American, was probably starstruck and reduced the speeding charge to the lesser one of careless operation of a vehicle. The sentence was a compromise. The prosecutor actually wanted to drop the charge

First love Rebecca DeMornay appeared with Tom in his first blockbuster movie, *Risky Business*. (©Archive Photos, Pictorial Parade)

On his way to a Hollywood premiere, Tom seems to be enjoying the success of his latest movie *Risky Business*. (©Kevin Winter/DMI)

Cruise, with "Brat Packers" Emilio Estevez and Rob Lowe at a 1982 Beverly Hills film screening. (©Archive Photos, Fotos International)

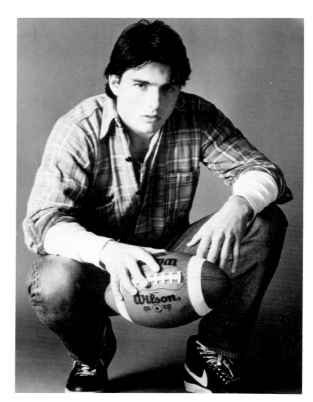

In 1983, Tom played a high school football player in the movie *All the Right Moves*. (©Retrophoto)

All the right moves to make it as a model.
(©Retrophoto)

A 1985 photoshoot of Tom Cruise.
(©Retrophoto)

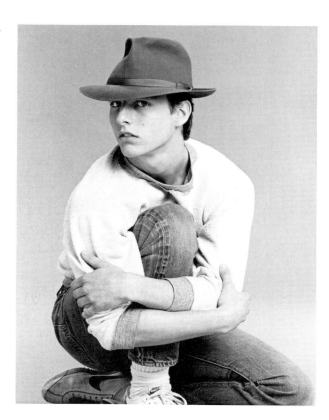

Together with Rebecca
De Mornay, his co-star in
*Risky Business*.
(©Ann Clifford/DMI)

America's new teen sensation: Tom
Cruise, on his way to another
movie premiere.
(©Kevin Winter/DMI)

Tom Cruise out on the town with his first wife Mimi Rogers. (©Kevin Winter/DMI and ©Retrophoto, David McGough)

Tom Cruise and his
trademark smile.
(©Archive Photos, Express Newspapers)

His role as ace fighter pilot
Maverick in *Top Gun* marked
Tom's "take-off" from film star
to movie icon.
(©Fotos International)

Despite their steamy romance
in the film, Tom and *Top Gun*
co-star Kelly McGillis did not
hit it off well on the set.
(©Archive Photos, Pictorial Parade)

Paul Newman gives his young protégé a lesson in pool-hustling in *The Color of Money*. (©Archive Photos)

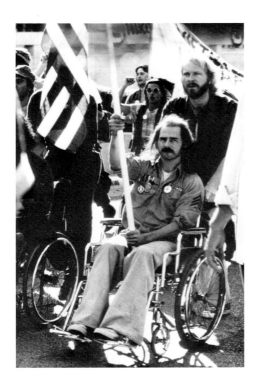

In *Born on the Fourth of July*, Tom portrayed disabled Vietnam War veteran Ron Kovic. He won a Golden Globe best actor award for the role in 1989.
(©Ron Neveu, Fotos International)

Although his career was on a high after being nominated for an Academy Award for *Born on the Fourth of July*, his personal life hit a low, when Tom Cruise divorced Mimi Rogers.
(©Kevin Winter/DMI)

After shooting his movie *Rainman*, Tom enjoys a night out with wife Mimi Rogers and fellow actors Goldie Hawn and Kurt Russell.
(©Albert Ferreira/DMI)

Tom Cruise and Dustin Hoffman both starred in *Rainman*, voted best picture at the 1989 Oscars. (©Kevin Winter/DMI)

Hoffman had long been Cruise's favorite actor, and the two built up a relationship of mutual respect on the set of *Rainman*. (©Archive Photos, Fotos International)

After seeing her in the Australian hit *Dead Calm*, Cruise knew Kidman would be his perfect co-star not only in *Days of Thunder*, but in his personal life as well.
(©Stephen Vaughan, Archive Photos)

Tom has found happiness with his second wife, Nicole Kidman.
(©Kevin Winter/DMI and Retrophoto)

A grimy Cruise steps out of his stock car in the 1989 *Days of Thunder*. (©Archive Photos)

Cruise addresses a crowd at an Earth Day rally in Washington, D.C. in April 1990.
(©Howard Sachs, Archive Photos.)

Gushing fans scramble to get a closer look at Tom in front of Hollywood's Grauman's Chinese Theater.
(©Miranda Shen, Fotos International)

Tom and Nicole wave to the crowd after Tom has added his hand and footprints to the sidewalk in front of Grauman's Chinese Theater in Hollywood.
(©Archive Photos)

Thomas Cruise Mapother IV today.
(©Alex Oliveira/DMI)

As a young Irish adventurer in 1992's *Far and Away*, Tom thunders on horseback to stake his claim in the nineteenth-century Oklahoma Land Rush.
(©Philip Caruso, Archive Photos)

Tom confronts Jack Nicholson as a military lawyer in a dramatic court-room scene from *A Few Good Men*, released in 1992.
(©Sidney Baldwin, Fotos International)

Tom starred in the 1993 legal thriller *The Firm*, based on the bestselling novel by John Grisham. Grisham thought Cruise was the perfect choice for the role.
(©Fotos International).

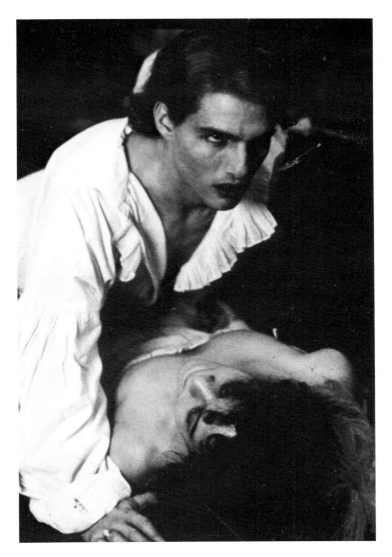

Cruise sinks his teeth into his role as Lestat in the film adaptation of Anne Rice's novel, *Interview with a Vampire*.
(©Fotos International)

Proud new adoptive parents Tom and Nicole appeared together at the 1993 Golden Globe awards. Cruise has starred with Kidman in both *Days of Thunder* and *Far and Away*.
(©Bob Grant, Archive Photos)

Dad looks both ways before crossing the street on a stroll with daughter Isabella.
(©Mitchell Gerber, LGI Photo Agency)

Nicole and Tom find time to relax on the playground with their daughter.
(©Mitchell Gerber, LGI Photo Agency)

altogether, but he feared word might leak out about lenient treatment of a movie star.

Cruise had more positive adventures on the road in Daytona Beach, Florida, another location for *Days of Thunder*. Although the story sounds like something concocted by a press agent working overtime, it comes not from the actor's flack but from his limo driver, Dave Garris, hired to chauffeur the star from his hotel to the set.

Garris recalled that one day Cruise shouted from the back seat, "Dave, pull over," even though they were speeding along the freeway. The sharp-eyed actor had spotted a homeless man on the shoulder of the road.

Risking life and limb on the freeway as cars whizzed past, Cruise got out of the car and approached the luckless man, who was holding a sign that said, "Will work for food."

Maybe the vagrant's plea touched off painful memories from Cruise's childhood when his mother had to apply for food stamps but was too embarrassed to use them. Or maybe he remembered being so hungry himself during his youth that he would wolf down all the food on his plate so his sisters wouldn't steal his portion. Whatever motivated Cruise, he obviously hadn't forgotten his roots. While many other self-made men try to bury their modest backgrounds and even make up more impressive pasts, Cruise remembered what it was like to be hungry and have no way of satiating that hunger.

He promptly emptied his pockets of all the cash he had on him, about $100. The startled vagrant, who was probably used to getting spare change or a dollar bill when he got any charity at all, must have been shocked at his sudden windfall. Cruise grabbed the scabby-looking man's hand with both of his and shook it heartily. "Take care," he said to the stunned transient before whisking off to another universe, so far away from the vagrant's and Cruise's own childhood poverty.

It wasn't just the desperately destitute who could pull at

Cruise's generous heartstrings. During another break in filming, Cruise was dining at a restaurant when he noticed a group of teenagers at a nearby table. The youngsters were obviously prom-goers, decked out in tuxedos, ballgowns, and corsages. Cruise recalled his own bittersweet prom, when he bought a suit two sizes too large so he could wear it for a long time after the one-night event. He went to the prom in a $100 suit, but the expense was squandered by the ill-fitting garment, which made him look like a dork, not an elegant gentleman.

Cruise motioned to his waiter, whispered something in his ear, then disappeared. When the teenagers, ten in all, later asked for the bill, they were told that "Mr. Cruise" had paid for all of them.

The empathetic actor was not only generous with cash, which he had a surplus of. He could also be generous with his time, a much more valuable commodity for a superstar in constant demand for moviemaking and charity fundraising.

Cruise took time off from spinning laps at the Charlotte, North Carolina, Speedway during *Days of Thunder* to visit Brandi Mason, who was dying of myocarditis, a rare viral infection of the heart. It was a particularly dicey time for the youngster. The only thing that could save her from certain death was a heart transplant. And so far, a suitable donor had not yet been found.

Cruise showed up at her hospital room, not with a donor heart, although you get the feeling he would have paid the estimated $125,000 a heart cost if he had been able to find one. Instead, he gave the girl a hat and a shirt and autographed her pillowcase. Brandi's mother Ginger remembered the visit like a divine apparition. "When he came into the room, her heart monitor showed her heart rate went up to 170 beats per minute," Ginger recalled, not seeming to mind the potentially lethal effects of the superstar's visit. "Brandi was absolutely so excited she couldn't stand it." The girl eventually found a suitable donor. And Cruise, although he was working fourteen-hour days, found time to visit the other pint-sized patients in the Charlotte hospital's children's ward.

Cruise got to play Florence Nightingale again in Charlotte, but this time the stakes were even higher and more personal. The actor loves to have his family visit the set of all his movies, which turns into a nice, all-expense-paid vacation to fabulous locales like Ireland and Versailles. His sister, Lee Anne, however, may have wished she had stayed home instead of accompanying her brother and her two-year-old son to Charlotte when the child got caught in a revolving door at their hotel. Tom played paramedic this time and rushed the toddler to the hospital emergency room, holding his hand while the doctor stitched up the other one, joking with the terrified child and generally being a great uncle. A relative speculated that Cruise was such a great uncle to his sisters' kids because he sorely missed a father figure during his own childhood. When Cruise tore a tendon during wrestling practice in high school, it was mom, not his absent dad, who took him to the hospital.

The "wrap" party to celebrate the end of filming also demonstrated Cruise's largesse. A teetotaller himself, the star picked up the tab for all the food and booze, an expense traditionally borne by the studio.

*Days of Thunder*, although not doing much for Tom's career, did impact dramatically on his personal life. For on the set of the film, amid crashing cars and bad dialogue, he met the love of his life, the future Mrs. Tom Cruise II. But first there was the original Mrs. Cruise to see to. How Cruise dealt with this "inconvenient woman" revealed a previously unseen side of his nice-guy personality. His callous regard for his wife's feelings was a shock to his acquaintances and colleagues who knew him only as the gallant who put his women on a pedestal. Maybe it says something about the mesmerizing power his future wife exerted over him that he for once abandoned his courtly ways and turned into an id-driven sex machine.

The farewell party for the film was the turning point. He didn't invite his wife to the event. Mimi had always shown up for such parties in the past, and the crew got the first inkling that all was not right at Casa Cruise. He had been so discreet with Kidman on the set that no one involved in the film had a clue that the co-stars were falling in love off screen as well as on.

Cruise was not so subtle with his wife, however. When she showed up on the set after finishing her own film, the flop *The Desperate Hours* in Los Angeles, Cruise welcomed her with closed arms. "I'm with Nicole now," he said tersely to his wife and asked for a divorce.

Rogers may have seen the split coming, and her belated arrival on the set could have been a futile act of desperation. It didn't work. From the beginning, the marriage didn't exactly seem doomed, but it had too many obstacles to overcome.

The eight-year age difference *per se* didn't damage the relationship. Cruise liked older women. Even Kidman, though not old enough to play a brain surgeon, looked a great deal more mature than her twenty-two years when they first tooled around the track together and jumped out of airplanes on the set of *Days of Thunder*. But the age difference between Cruise and Rogers had more significance than sexual allure. Rogers actually behaved like the younger partner in the marriage. She was a party girl who liked to go club-hopping with friends like Kirstie Alley in West Hollywood. Cruise has always seemed an old man in a younger man's body, and in his twenties, when counterparts like Charlie Sheen were tearing up the town, Cruise was happy to cocoon at home with a video and a like-minded partner, which Rogers manifestly was not.

Their two-career marriage also caused problems, but not ones you might expect. Rogers, not nearly so obsessed with her career as her husband was with his, appeared willing to subordinate her needs to her husband's. Six months after their marriage

in 1987, Rogers would provide a hint of why the marriage ultimately failed.

"If I were offered an unbelievable role that was shooting in
Tunisia for three or four months and Tom couldn't go...well,
Tunisia would have to wait. Those long separations are too high
a price to pay. You can't put a relationship through such stress.
Tom is as committed as I am. This is for real."

Unfortunately, her resolve *wasn't* for real. She ignored her
own philosophy of marriage and left Cruise in North Carolina
while she shot *The Desperate Hours* in L.A.

Who can say? If she had accompanied Cruise to the North
Carolina location *before* the wrap party, as she had faithfully
done in the past, the gentlemanly actor might not have been
tempted by his nubile co-star, Kidman.

But Rogers was out of sight, out of mind, and her husband
ended up in somebody else's arms.

The failure of the marriage didn't have anything to do with
competitiveness. They weren't starring in an updated *A Star Is
Born*, as Rogers career went nowhere and Cruise's went through
the roof. In a still unliberated society like ours, it has traditionally been easier for a woman to tolerate her husband's greater
success than vice versa.

Rogers said as much when she admitted, "Being married to
Tom Cruise didn't hurt my career. But it certainly didn't help it.
Nobody hires you because you're married to somebody famous.
In fact, I think you're tested a little more because of it."

Rogers, of course, is being disingenuous here. There was a
huge publicity barrage for another one of her flops, *Someone to
Watch Over Me*, and not because her co-star was B-list actor
Tom Berenger or the director was Ridley Scott, who hadn't had
a commercial hit since *Alien* and who had almost destroyed
Cruise's career with *Legend*. Rogers must have felt truly cursed
when she starred with an A-list actor like Denzel Washington
in *The Mighty Quinn* since that film was one of his few flops.

You don't have to be terribly cynical to realize that *Someone to Watch Over Me* received special notice because it starred Mrs. Tom Cruise.

"The only way that marriage might have affected my career is that if you decide your marriage is your first priority, then your career will suffer. Had I been unmarried and focused on my career, maybe things would have gone faster," Rogers said.

More disingenuity there. Presumably, she had been focused before she met Cruise, and even then her career was going nowhere—unless you count starring in a short-lived series, *Paper Dolls*, playing a bimbo mannequin as "going somewhere."

More important than any career rivalry, however, was the basic sexual incompatibility of the two sexy stars. Cruise was sexy on screen. So sexy, he has a standing (or should we say reclining) offer from the editor of *Playgirl* to doff his duds in the pages of the magazine any time he wants to. *Playgirl*'s editor Nancie Martin summed up the attractiveness of his many parts. "That smile, those eyes—and he's muscular in all the right places."

Off screen, to paraphase Carole Lombard's comment about *her* husband, Clark Gable, Rogers might have said, "Cruise is no Cruise."

Mimi liked to party. Tom liked to cocoon. Mimi had a healthy appetite for sex and was something of an exhibitionist, as her full frontal nudity in *Playboy* showed.

Tom had a different attitude toward sex.

He didn't want any.

At least that was his ex-wife's take on the subject in the text accompanying those revealing shots in *Playboy*.

Much more titillating than her ample breasts or unclothed crotch were her comments about the "monastery" that was their home. Rogers, however, was an unwilling nun at Cruise Abbey.

More important than baring her body was Rogers's need to bare the intimate details of her marriage with Cruise. The actress also took the opportunity between photos to absolve herself of any culpability in the breakup.

"Is that the story, that I was bored with that child and threw him over, chewed him up and spit him out?" she asked the *Playboy* interviewer.

"Shall we let that be story?" she added Socratically, immediately answering her own question with a resounding "no way."

"Here's the real story. Tom was seriously thinking of becoming a monk. At least for that period of time, it looked as though the marriage wouldn't fit into his overall spiritual need, and he thought he had to be celibate to maintain the purity of his instrument."

Cruise's reason for depriving his frustrated wife was apparently based on a ridiculously out-of-date theory about sublimating one's sexual urges in another channel. This bastardized Freudian theory led prizefighters for years to go without sex before the big bout so they could release all their pent-up sexual energy on their opponent in the ring. Football players followed the same debunked theory.

And so, to the ruin of his marriage, did Thomas Mapother Cruise IV, much to his sexy wife's distress.

As she explained in her spread for *Playboy*, Tom wanted to keep his instrument pure, "My instrument, on the other hand, needs tuning."

Sublimating your sex drive into your work is a hoary old theory that has been largely discredited. In fact, one study of football players found that a little sex the night before the big game actually relaxed them and allowed them to play a better game.

Psychologist Kate Wachs believes this kind of sexual sublimation does work, but only up to a point. If you overdo it with total abstinence, she maintains, you're asking for trouble.

"A certain amount of abstinence before the game or fight is good, but after a while it is not good if you're totally frustrated.

But it's good to be a *little* frustrated. You take that energy and turn it into something creative. That's a Freudian concept, but it does work sometimes. Most people relax after having sex, and therefore you don't have the energy or drive to put in a good performance. If you're more edgy, a little tense and anxious, that's good for your performance. For a while anxiety helps, but after a certain point it makes your performance worse because you're too anxious and distracted from what you want to do," Dr. Wachs says.

As looney as Rogers's allegations were, her husband's sublimation, if that indeed was what was going on, apparently worked. During this infertile marriage, Cruise enjoyed some of the most fertile work of his career, working with big-name directors in prestige productions that didn't include a single soaring plane or squealing car, unless you count the Porsche in *Rainman*.

Whatever burnished Cruise's career, he had found the right formula. Over the course of three films, he went from bankable pretty boy to Oscar contender and best friend of cranky, older superstars. And these prestige pictures, like the previous popcorn pics, gobbled up the box office too.

Meanwhile, Mimi Rogers had not been so fortunate.

In the *Playboy* interview, Rogers had said she would like to star in a remake of the 1952 film *The Bad and the Beautiful*. That hasn't happened, and with her lack of clout, her name doesn't have the marquee value to get the project off the ground.

After the divorce (in January 1990), however, Rogers suggested that sexual incompatibility wasn't the only thing that drove a stake through the heart of the marriage. *US* magazine asked her what turned her off in a man, and her reply sounded like a thumbnail sketch of her ex-husband's driven personality.

"A man who is compulsive or obsessive in any way gets very annoying. Or else the stiff-upper-lip school of never showing what you feel," Rogers said.

Cruise was guilty on both counts. His obsessiveness about nailing down a role, whether it involved living in a wheelchair or driving a racecar like a pro, was already well documented. His stiff upper lip became evident in his dealings with the press.

Even after he had separated from Rogers and was about to begin divorce proceedings, he lied to reporters about the state of his marriage. In a Christmas cover story in *Time* magazine to promote *Born on the Fourth of July*, he stared *Time* film critic Richard Corliss straight in the face and said, "The most important thing for me is I want Mimi to be happy."

Strictly speaking, Cruise didn't lie to the powerful film critic for the most influential magazine in the country. Maybe he felt Mimi would be happier not married to him. He did lie, however, to *Rolling Stone* and *US*, when he told them, "I couldn't imagine being without her or being alone. I just really enjoy our marriage."

By that time, the couple had already separated.

*Time*'s Corliss was not amused at being made a laughingstock and dupe of the superstar. The respected critic later said, "His was an Academy Award-worthy performance. Apparently he gave it to all the reporters. Every celebrity plays a game. Tom Cruise was giving one of his best performances by playing Tom Cruise."

A few weeks after the cover story in *Time*, Cruise finally came clean. His *mea culpa* wasn't very convincing. His publicist put out the following statement on behalf of her client: "This has been a time when I have been the focus of much attention. When I was asked direct questions by the press about my marriage, I felt that to compromise our privacy was to compromise a basic trust. I hope that can be understood."

Although Cruise was too much of a gentleman to begin an affair with Kidman while still married to Rogers, it didn't stop him from chastely courting his leading lady and lavishing gifts on her.

His Harley or BMW would often be spotted parked outside Kidman's condo on location in Daytona Beach. The two were seen dining at the trendy Olive Garden there. They went for hamburger meat and other barbecue fare at Publix Market.

Even more romantically, he took his future wife skydiving and bought her two parachutes that cost $5,000. This had to be done very discreetly. Not only because he didn't want to embarrass his estranged wife, but also because the insurers of *Days of Thunder* absolutely forbade such a dangerous pastime. (As if racing cars at 182 miles per hour without a stunt double wasn't dangerous enough!)

Cruise may indeed be sexually stifled, as his disgruntled first wife claimed, but he is romantic in an old fashioned way that is more appealing to women than saying, "Hey, babe! Wanna come back to my place and do a superstar?"

While hurtling to the earth at 110 miles per hour, Cruise swooped over to Kidman and planted a kiss on her in mid-air. Tellingly, as an Easter present, he later took his mother skydiving and kissed her en route to the ground as well.

By March it was public knowledge that Mimi was out and Nicole was in when he accompanied Kidman to the 1990 Academy Awards. Again, he took his mother along, plus his siblings. After the divorce, Cruise remained his usual gentlemanly self. He had his publicist put out a statement explaining—barely—the reasons they had split. "While there have been very positive aspects to our marriage, there were some issues which could not be resolved even after working on them for a period of time," they said in a joint statement, suggesting a certain amicableness to the divorce, at least until the *Playboy* interview. Later, he would confess to Barbara Walters on prime-time TV that he and the ex-Mrs. Cruise were no longer speaking. But still the gentleman, he added, "I wish her well."

For her part, Rogers seemed relieved about the failure of her marriage, although failure was a word she insisted wasn't in her vocabulary. She said, "If your partner decides he's leaving, there's not a whole lot you can do. That doesn't make you a failure at marriage. I'd do it again."

In the meantime, she's living with a Tom Cruise look-alike, only taller, by the name of Chris Ciaffa, a production assistant she met on the set of a cable movie. They share a handsome Brentwood house—paid for by Tom Cruise as part of the divorce settlement.

While Rogers consoles herself in the handsome arms of her production assistant, she claims she's happy that the Mrs. Tom Cruise spotlight now shines on another woman. "Now (Nicole) takes the heat much more than I do. It puts most of the burden on her, which makes me happy. I don't mean that in a mean way, but Tom and I are divorced. We haven't been together in two years. I deserve to have that name go away."

While Cruise was romancing his co-star on the set of *Days of Thunder*, he was at the same time typically charming his new father figure, Robert Duvall, who played the pit-crew chief. Duvall realized the off-camera role he was being asked to play when he discussed his protégé's work ethic. "Tom's father wasn't around. I guess he grew up having to prove something on his own. I'm sure it's something of a catalyst. It drives you farther into new areas. To prove some things," Duvall said.

At Christmas, a year after the two men had completed filming and gone their separate ways, Cruise was still enamored of his latest mentor and bought Duvall a jumping horse. Cost: $25,000.

Cruise didn't charm producer Don Simpson on the set, however. After the *New Republic's* film critic Stanley Kaufman complained that Cruise's voice was too thin and high pitched in *Born on the Fourth of July*, Cruise became obsessed with correcting the "problem." If he had too much baby fat for a role, he could pump iron. If he was too short for a leading lady, elevator shoes could take care of the height inequality.

His squeaky voice, however, required a more high-tech

solution. Once again, the Church of Scientology, which he claimed helped him deal with misdiagnosed dyslexia, came to the rescue with a sound recording system invented by a Church member. It was called ClearSound, it was exceedingly expensive, and Cruise wanted it to thicken his vocal chords.

The conventional recording system, in use with variations since the advent of the talkies, cost about $5,000. The souped up ClearSound cost a whopping $100,000. That's still chicken feed on a movie with a budget of $60 or $70 million, but Don Simpson had almost as much clout as Cruise, since he had made blockbusters like *Beverly Hills Cop*, *Flash Dance*, and *Top Gun*. When Scientology's high school dropout "Pope," David Miscavige, showed up on the set pushing ClearSound, Simpson told the church leader "no way." And when a senior member of the Church reiterated his boss's request, saying, "Tom would be very happy if you used ClearSound," Simpson said to the church official, "Your church is full of crap."

While muckraking *Spy* magazine claimed ClearSound was a "squeak-suppressing system," Cruise claimed "all it is is a recording system" that electronically enhances all the sound in the movie, not just a certain superstar's soprano. Uncharacteristically, Cruise denounced the *Spy* story as "bullshit."

Simpson thought ClearSound, at twenty times the cost of the existing sound system, prohibitively expensive. The producer had the temerity to overrule his star and make his wishes stick. The result is that you can hear Cruise's high-pitched voice throughout *Days of Thunder*.

For Simpson's part, crossing his star was a case of being penny-wise and pound-foolish, tons of "pounds" foolish. The two men, after collaborating on almost half a billion dollars worth of moviemaking, never worked together again. Simpson's imperiousness cost him big, a lot more than the difference between a $5,000 and $100,000 sound system. For when it came time to make *Top Gun II*, the star of the original was suddenly unavailable. Simpson, along with partner Jerry Bruckheimer, had a deal to make the sequel for Paramount. Their fee would be $2 million. With Cruise off the project, Paramount offered them a measly $750,000 to do the sequel with Cher's former boy toy, Val Kilmer. Enraged, Simpson and company stormed off the backlot of Paramount and into the welcoming arms of Mickey Mouse.

It was a disastrous move.

The freewheeling Simpson found himself the odd man out at Disney, the most controlling studio in town. So notorious for its mistreatment of talent and staff, the lot has been nicknamed "Mauschwitz" and "Duckau."

After landing in the Magic Kingdom in 1991, the power-house team of Simpson and Bruckheimer took four years to produce a film. At Paramount, they cranked out an average of one blockbuster per year.

No one has ever accused Tom Cruise of being vindictive, but as he watches the decline of Simpson's career and his own ascension, he may reflect on the Spanish proverb: "Revenge is a dish best served cold."

However, although Cruise hasn't deigned to work with Simpson again, his generosity toward his former colleague is typically Cruise-like. After making *Days of Thunder*, Cruise gave Simpson a macho but thoughtful gift, and a very expensive one. He paid the $25,000 tuition for a course in racecar driving for his cantankerous producer since Simpson had had so much fun playing a bit part in the film, typecast as an egomaniacal racing star.

Cruise gave himself the same gift, attending the school with Simpson. While he was willing to sit in the classroom with the imperious Simpson, he would never work with his erstwhile mentor on a film set again.

Is Tom Cruise vindictive? His $25,000 thank you to Simpson suggests he doesn't hold a grudge. And he hasn't worked with a lot of people more than once, including the objects of his idol worship, Newman and Hoffman.

Still, Newman and Hoffman don't tend to appear in the big-budget action films Cruise loves. Simpson and Bruckheimer, if they ever escape Mauschwitz, do.

One wonders if Simpson ever wakes up on sweaty Porthault sheets in the middle of the night in his Bel Air mansion and says to himself, "If only I had spent a few extra bucks on that damn sound system...!"

# TWELVE

# Mrs. Tom Cruise: The Sequel

**W**hen Nicole Kidman arrived in America in 1989 to star in *Days of Thunder*, she was an unknown in the US, but on her home continent she was a star. While still in high school, she had won the Australian equivalent of an Oscar and Emmy for playing a student who becomes a Vietnam War protester in the 1986 miniseries, *Vietnam*. Three years later, she starred in a low-budget thriller, *Dead Calm*, which became one of the biggest hits in the history of the Australian film industry. It was also the film that made Tom Cruise fall a little bit in love with a woman he had seen only on screen.

While Cruise fell in love with the celluloid image of the woman he would later marry, it took his future wife a little bit longer—but not much longer. In fact, she later would say it was love at first sight on her part. Kidman had of course seen his films, but it wasn't until she met him in person that her feelings became mutual. "The very first time we met, I discovered what a charming and tender man he is. He must be every woman's dream," she cooed.

When Kidman was summoned to America by the prince of Hollywood to star in *Days of Thunder*, she gladly obeyed the royal command.

Like her future husband, she also had some emotional baggage to discard before embarking on her career as Mrs. Tom Cruise II. Her "baggage," however, was more successful than Cruise's. He was her live-in boyfriend, a drop-dead gorgeous Aussie soap star named Graham Chapman. When Kidman embarked for America, the handsome couple were still very much an item. And Chapman had the long-distance phone bill to prove it. In an interview after his girlfriend dumped him for Cruise, Chapman remembered ruefully that he spent hundreds of dollars calling her on the set of *Days of Thunder*. He could have saved his dimes. By the time *Days of Thunder* wrapped, *People* magazine sardonically reported, "Kidman was going around the track with Cruise."

Broken-hearted even before the breakup, Chapman said, "Being separated from Nicole is very difficult. She is not just my girl, she is also my best friend." Curiously, that is the same term Cruise would later use to describe his romantic relationship with Kidman.

Chapman, for all his looks, was no match for America's reigning superstar. Kidman found herself strongly attracted to her kind consort's physical charms. "Tom has a fantastic face and the cutest smile in the world," Kidman said.

For his part, Cruise must have been stunned by his future wife's physical allure since he invited her to America after merely seeing her image on screen.

In person, Kidman was the living embodiment of Miss Drew, the heroine of *Billy Bathgate*, a role she would later play. Without knowing the actress who would play his creation on screen, E.L. Doctorow in his best-selling novel described Miss Drew as "so blindingly beautiful under that cut gold hair. Her eyes were so green and her skin so white, it was like trying to look into the sun. You couldn't see her through the brilliance and it hurt to try for more than an instant."

Cruise could have written those words himself for he was indeed blinded by his leading lady's beauty. Unlike Doctorow, who could only describe such beauty in words, Cruise could pick up the phone and summon the real thing in the flesh all the way from Down Under.

Nicole Kidman came from a world that was not only geographically far from Cruise's, socio-economically and emotionally, her upbringing was everything her future husband's was not. She was not the child of divorce. Her parents were well-heeled professionals and still married. And maybe because her childhood was relatively untroubled compared to Cruise's formative years of poverty and dislocation, Kidman had a much lighter take on life.

"Nicole's a kidder and brings that out in Tom. He laughs more when he's around her. Nicole's a little giddier and more fun-loving than Tom is. I think she brings out some of that in Tom. She would be laughing and joking, and he would be smiling and laughing more when he was with her," said *Days of Thunder*'s cinematographer, Ward Russell, a man who should know since he spent months looking through a lens at the smitten couple.

Cruise would later confirm that observation, saying, "Nic just makes me feel fun around her."

Nicole's father is Dr. Anthony Kidman, a biologist and psychologist who still lives in Nicole's hometown of Sydney with her mother, Janelle, a nurse. It's a close-knit family, professionally and emotionally. Mom edits Dad's psychology books and articles. They raised their two daughters in an affluent suburb of Sydney. In fact, one published account says the Kidmans are one of the ten richest families in Australia.

Although the Kidmans were several rungs, maybe a whole flight of stairs, higher up on the socio-economic ladder, Dr. Kidman and Tom's mother had one interesting thing in common. Both taught learning disabled children, specializing in hyperkinetic and dyslexic youngsters.

Despite a happier and more stable childhood, Kidman grew up with a poor body image and feelings of self-loathing just as Tom did. While Cruise had to contend with being below-average height in a world where tall men statistically live longer and do better financially, Kidman had just the opposite problem: she was a geeky teen who towered over classmates at 5'10".

While Tom thought his smile was "off" during his adolescence, Kidman had a more severe dysmorphic body image. "I thought I was the ugliest girl in the world until the guys started asking me out on dates," she said as though waking up from a nightmare.

Whatever remaining insecurity she clung to as an adult must have been totally banished when the most handsome movie star in the world called and said he wanted her to be in his next picture.

Before she met Cruise, Kidman obsessed over her height.

"I was a skinny, gawky, freckle-faced thing. I wasn't able to play Mary in the school Christmas play because I was so tall. Instead I played a sheep. I cried my eyes out."

It's interesting to note that this future screen beauty and her hunk of a husband both felt unattractive or downright ugly during their formative years. Their drive and ambition, necessary in the cutthroat, competitive world of acting, is no doubt fueled by childhood feelings of inadequacy.

As much as Kidman hated the way she looked, she felt even worse about her voice. That's something else she shared with Cruise, who was desperate to use ClearSound as a way to make his voice sound more manly.

Kidman remembered cringing in the theater when she first heard herself on screen. "I was shocked. I couldn't believe it was me walking about in that stupid way and speaking in a voice that I would never have imagined."

Maybe it was bad "tapes," as fellow Scientologists like to call memories, from her geeky childhood that haunted her, but in the here and now she felt her height could be a problem for her career. "I used to think I'd never be able to work in the movies because all male actors are short," said Kidman, who had apparently never bumped into six-foot-plus actors Chevy Chase or Clint Eastwood at Spago. "But now I've worked with Dustin Hoffman and Tom, and they're both shorter than me. So I'm fine about my height... now," she added. (During her starving actress days, Geena Davis used to tell casting directors she was 5'12", and no one apparently ever caught on that she was a towering six-footer.)

Even with the height handicap, Kidman has demonstrated that she can flourish away from her husband's prodigious shadow.

Kidman had mixed feelings about leaving Australia, where she was an award-winning actress, and moving to the US, where she was a nobody, except in Cruise's estimation. It wasn't simply that she went from being a big frog in a small pond to a small frog in a huge pond, Kidman hated Los Angeles. In 1989, she said, "I wouldn't want to live in LA. I think you could get very lonely."

It's proof of her infatuation with Cruise that she would later say, "Home is wherever my husband is."

Still, unlike Rogers—and maybe this is the secret of the success of Cruise's second marriage—Kidman was not content being the "little woman," figuratively or literally, following her husband from set to set while her own career withered.

Rogers had said that she'd pass up a good role to be with her husband. Kidman was a thoroughly modern career woman who would dump hubby—temporarily—to work halfway around the world for a juicy part.

Kidman also felt the same way about her husband's career needs. "If it's a great film, I'm not going to tell him that he can't work... *and vice versa*," she said with the same resolution with which she dispatched a serial murderer in *Dead Calm*.

A liberated man of the '90s, Cruise actually found his wife's independence and frankness a turn on. "What attracts me about a woman? Well, an Australian accent, red hair, blue eyes. I like someone who's independent. The thing about Nic is that she has her own career. It challenges me. I like someone who is going to keep the relationship going and make it fun. Someone who's very honest. There's nothing unsaid," he said.

Although Cruise has shown he's willing to take a risk and stretch in a wheelchair or a vampire's coffin, Kidman is even more adventurous than her skydiving, racecar-crashing husband. Cruise has said on more than one occasion he won't do a nude scene. Kidman already has.

In *Billy Bathgate* she went topless. And she campaigned for the role that went to Demi Moore in *Indecent Proposal* even though her husband had turned down the Woody Harrelson part because he felt the movie's concept—a man sells his wife to billionaire Robert Redford for a one-night stand in return for a cool million—morally repugnant.

Unlike her puritanical husband, the Australian actress has a more European attitude toward nudity. The Riviera is famous, for among other things, it's nude beaches, and dancers routinely flash their breasts on a German TV gameshow called *Tutti Frutti*. In the wee hours of the night, an Italian variety show invites housewives to strip on the air. It's the highest rated show in a land that also gave us the Pope.

When Kidman explains her philosophy on film nudity, she proves you can be a feminist and an exhibitionist at the same time. "I'm not one of those who say I'd *never* take off my clothes, that it's a terrible thing," she said at the press junket for *Far and Away*. "I've done it, and it's fine as long as the nudity isn't gratuitous instead of some director or writer getting his rocks off." Unlike her husband, Kidman employs colorful language that would make Cruise blush.

"A lot of directors are flat-out misogynists. They treat women as second-class citizens. I do object to having nudity and violence together, like a woman being beaten or cut up. But lovemaking on screen? I haven't got anything against that at all."

Obviously Kidman has come a long way—politically—
from her childhood when she coveted a Barbie doll. It wasn't a
matter of money, since the family was well off. It was her feminist mother's objections to Barbie's, well, Barbie-doll image that
kept the bouffant-hairdoed mannequin out of the house.

Cruise dropped out of *Bright Lights, Big City* because he
felt it glorified drugs. More inexplicably, he nixed *Rush*, although that film's chronicle of two cops going to hell on cocaine
hardly glorified the drug life.

Unlike her G-rated husband, Kidman described her *laissez-
faire* attitude toward the subject thus: "I have nothing against
sex or nudity on screen."

A reporter once asked if the couple had the same rule that
governed another power couple, Bruce Willis and Demi Moore,
on screen philandering: no French kissing unless you're married
to your co-star. Kidman laughed and said, "No tongue? No, no.
It's like you're an actor. And if you're doing something you
believe in and aren't embarrassed about, that's appropriate for
the character. I wouldn't put those limitations on Tom, and I
wouldn't expect him to put them on me. There *are* some things
I won't do." Pressed on that, Kidman declined to be specific. "I
can't say. There are just certain things I feel are not what I consider a good role model for women."

Cruise separated from his first wife early in 1990. As soon
as the complicated but not messy divorce was finalized in the
fall, he wasted precious little time marrying the second Mrs.
Cruise on Christmas Eve, 1990, in Telluride, Colorado.

The wedding this time around was more formal, in keeping with the groom's maturity. He had married Mimi when he
was all of twenty-five, and it was a hippie-ish wedding with
bride and groom wearing matching jeans and no shoes.

Three years later, at twenty-eight, Cruise was feeling more
traditional. And he felt like spending more money. For the hush-
hush ceremony, he rented a $2-million, six-bedroom log cabin

with a spectacular view of the Rockies. The spacious house was filled with fragrant flower arrangements in the dead of winter. Although she was only twenty-two, Kidman was also bitten by the formality bug. She wore a traditional white gown with a long train. Cruise for once took off his jeans and torn T-shirt and donned a tuxedo. A civil servant conducted the ceremony, Nicole's younger sister, Antonia, was bridesmaid, and Dustin Hoffman was best man. The only note of informality was the wedding vows, which the bride and groom wrote themselves.

A nasty rumor hung over the ceremony—that Kidman was pregnant and the ceremony in Telluride was actually a shot-gun wedding. Her uncle, Barry Fawcett, came to his niece's defense and said, "They're married because they're in love. It's as simple as that." It was also pointed out that if Kidman had indeed been pregnant she wouldn't have continued to go skydiving with her daredevil husband. Together, they made ten jumps!

Cruise himself was gallant when he explained the real reason for their hasty marriage. "I think anybody who has met Nic would understand why we got married so quickly."

After the wedding, they immediately became the invisible couple when they weren't visible on screen. Kidman denied they had become Mr. and Mrs. Greta Garbo, the Jackie Onassis of celebrity couples. True, they never turned up at Spago or the Ivy or Morton's, watering holes *par excellence* for Los Angeles's glitterati. They still went out—just not to places where the paparazzi would descend on them like shutterbugging locusts.

Kidman insisted they were not isolated in the least. "You're kidding me," she told a magazine reporter when the Howard Hughes comparison was made. "We just went to Paris with six friends and went wild. I suppose it's because we don't go out to a lot of Hollywood things. We have lots of friends who just come over, play pool." Both Cruises are avid bowlers. As a wedding present, frugal best man Dustin Hoffman gave them his and her balls.

Until she moved to LA, Kidman didn't own a car. She insisted she would never own an expensive one, a promise she was unable to keep when her husband gave her a red Mercedes over her objections.

The car and the house are the only movie-star trappings they enjoy. Away from home, they like to melt into the crowd—as far as that's possible—and never demand red-carpet treatment. They don't hit the Bel Air circuit, where all the hot movies are screened in the homes of studio executives before the peons get to see them in theaters.

These "just folks" millionaires gladly join the ranks of the groundlings. "Nic and I go to the movies opening weekend. We get in line. We go shopping just like everybody else in the grocery store. There are times when you might get mobbed, but I find if I'm relaxed, I can handle the situation. You can become a prisoner of fame if you allow it do so. I don't want to live my life like that," Cruise has said.

They are also helped out by the fact that they live in Los Angeles. Fellow Los Angelenos seem to have an unwritten code: LA is the movie stars' home turf, and they deserve to be left alone.

When they stray outside the trendy confines of Los Angeles, however, it's open season on celebrities. But the resourceful Cruise's have even found a way around that. For a trip to Disneyland, Cruise wore wraparound sunglasses (not his signature *Risky Business* Ray-Bans) and a baseball cap. Nicole admitted she didn't need any disguise because her face isn't as famous as her photogenic husband's.

# THIRTEEN

# Not Far and Away Enough

In early 1992, the National Association of Theater Owners (NATO) made official what everyone in the film industry already conceded, that Tom Cruise was a box-office king. At its ShoWest convention in Las Vegas, NATO named him star of the year. Later, the avant-garde Chicago Film Festival would outdo the mercenary theater owners and proclaim Cruise "star of the decade." In his typical self-deprecating mode, Cruise wondered aloud if he was being honored for the past decade or the present one.

NATO's movie-house moguls had a special reason to love Tom Cruise. His films sold popcorn—literally. It's not common knowledge, but it's this buttery, over-priced treat that actually puts money in the pockets of theater owners. The lion's share of ticket sales goes to the movie studio. The theater owners' take of ticket revenue is consumed by overhead. Popcorn, Jujubees, and Milk Duds, though, are pure profit. And the more bodies a star can put in the theater per screening, the more popcorn is sold.

NATO's reps loved the popcorn-selling Cruise. By 1992 his movies had sold $1.6 billion worth of tickets and just as much in concessions to moviegoers.

Amid all the backslapping and profit counting, the theater owners might have yanked Cruise's award out of his hands if they had seen his next film, *Far and Away*. Fortunately for the awardee, *Far and Away* wouldn't crash and burn in theaters until later that summer. In January Cruise was still able to bask in the glow of the theater owners' approval.

Even more so than *Days of Thunder*, which at least looked good on paper, *Far and Away* proved again the maxim that a star who thinks he is an *auteur* is a scary thing. It's hard to imagine how Cruise and director Ron Howard pitched the low concept of the film to the tight-fisted executives at Universal. MCA-Universal president Sid Sheinberg's frugal cautiousness had been proved wrong when another low-concept Cruise baby, *Born on the Fourth of July*, burned up the box office and the Oscars, so this time he gave Cruise free rein.

Where was the authoritarian Louis B. Mayer when you needed him?

On paper and on screen, *Far and Away* was a costly turkey. Set in nineteenth-century Ireland and America, the original script followed the loves and losses of a star-crossed couple. He was a poor farmer who left the Old Sod to try for fame, fortune, and free land in the Oklahoma Land Rush. She was an aristocratic beauty who left her stately home to escape a loveless marriage. In America, the two would cross paths, cross hearts, and cross over into romance.

That's not, of course, how Cruise and Howard pitched the story to Universal. All they had to say about the project is "This film will star Tom Cruise," and the immovable Sid Sheinberg was sold. Left unsaid in the pitch and unnecessary was that there were 1.6 billion reasons to finance anything Tom Cruise wanted to do.

Universal should have known better. Eventually every bankable superstar goes bust. Call it the Eddie Murphy syndrome. Even the unbeatable Arnold Schwarzenegger got beaten into the ground with *Last Action Hero*, the *Heaven's Gate* of action movies. And Cruise wanted to do something even more perilous; he wanted to make a costume drama.

Until recently, Hollywood hated costume dramas. All those corsets and wigs, buckboards and rigs cost more than crashing cop cars or exploding high rises.

Plus, dynamiting real estate, no matter how pricey, appeals to the all important teenage movie demographic. Costume dramas only appeal to Academy voters and eggheads who don't go to the movies and get their jollies watching *Masterpiece Theater* and sending for transcripts of the *MacNeil-Lehrer Hour*.

Disney would later buy Merchant-Ivory after their costume dramas won one too many Oscars, but Merchant-Ivory at least made costume extravaganzas with unextravagant budgets under $10 million.

Cruise wanted to make his costume drama for $50 million, which meant that, after the usual excesses, the price would balloon to $70 million.

Sid Sheinberg probably hyperventilated with anticipation when he gave the studio's second Tom Cruise project the green light.

During the filming of *Far and Away*, Tom and his bride enjoyed a scenic honeymoon on the Emerald Isle—all expenses paid.

Cruise almost had to go on his honeymoon without his bride. When the superstar "suggested" to the film's director, Ron Howard, that he cast his wife opposite him, Howard disingenuously told Cruise he was unfamiliar with the lady or her work.

The gossip columnist for *Los Angeles* magazine laughed at Howard's claim that he didn't' know who Kidman was. "Howard is clearly in the loop somewhere *behind* a housewife in Podunk," the magazine's insider column smirked.

Brian Grazer, the film's producer, apparently pulled Howard aside and told him exactly who Kidman was. It's hard to believe that Howard didn't know Kidman was Mrs. Tom Cruise since their enraptured faces had graced every magazine cover from *People* to *The National Enquirer*.

Howard lamely explained, "Tom told me he liked working

with [Kidman], but he didn't tell me they were going together. I guess he kind of tricked us."

More likely, it was the affable, easy-going director's way of dissuading Cruise from using his wife in the film. No such luck. What Tom Cruise wants, Tom Cruise gets. And he wanted to spend his Irish honeymoon with his Australian bride.

By now, Cruise had perfected his *modus operandi* of the velvet glove concealing an iron fist. Instead of throwing a tantrum, Cruise arranged for Howard to screen several of Kidman's films.

Later in an interview, Howard would claim he was bowled over by Kidman's screen luminescence and was happy to cast her. More likely, he was bowled over by her husband's screen clout.

But where Howard genuinely perfected his passive-aggressive style of accommodating willful superstars was in his *detente* with the Church of Scientology. Mercifully, Ron Howard was no Don Simpson. "Opie" would never tell the Pope of Scientology to "fuck off" as Simpson had on the set of *Days of Thunder* when pressured to use the exorbitantly expensive ClearSound recording system.

A master of compromise, Howard used both sound systems, the cheap, venerable, and perfectly workable system that dated back to *The Jazz Singer* plus the $100,000 ClearSound. Peace reigned on the set, although you can almost imagine Scrooge Sheinberg back in his office punching $100,000 into his calculator. But at $50, er, $70 million, what was another measly hundred grand?

Uncharacteristically, Cruise finally exploded when one too many reporters hounded him about ClearSound. Even more atypically, he spewed out a string of profanities. "There's no such thing as a great Hollywood sound system. I've done enough looping in my life to know. The sound people in Hollywood are like a priesthood. They're from another era. No one usually gives a shit about sound. With a lot of [soundmen], it just pisses them off. And I say, 'Fuck you! OK, I want the best.' I simply found a system that's better. All I want is clarity on the voice. I don't think that's asking for so much, is it?"

Even if it were, by this point in his career, the studios were willing to give him anything he asked for. There was simply no such thing as "too much" with a possible payoff of half a billion dollars if *Far and Away* turned into another *Top Gun* money machine.

The bad press about ClearSound got so bad that the director felt compelled to defend his star against charges of rampaging ego in a *Spy* magazine article. "The thing that *Spy* got wrong is that Tom has something wrong with his voice. He never said this would lower his voice. He's an audiophile. He likes to have the latest sound gadgets—even in his car." Cruise even claimed the extremely expensive system would *not* enhance his voice, only "capture" it better.

Howard admitted he had had some doubts about using the system, but when he listened to the results in the editing room, he was delighted, and said, "It sounded really good. I think I'd like to use this system again."

As for the hundred grand *Spy* claimed Howard's company had to shell out to keep Cruise happy, Howard denied it and added this footnote about Cruise's generosity. "He gave us the equipment" for free, Howard said.

It was a shame that ClearSound couldn't change Cruise's ineradicable American accent. Clearly he was no Meryl Streep, who can switch from a Polish to a British to an Australian accent at the drop of a script. Cruise even admitted to *People* magazine that he was having a "divil" of a time with the inflections of Shaw and Joyce. But being the hard-working perfectionist he is, he hired not one but two dialect coaches and listened to recordings of Irish playwright Sean O'Casey to get the right brogue.

Cruise worked on his accent with as much industry as he trained for the boxing and land-rush scenes. "We had a great

accent coach," he said at the press junket for the film in Beverly
Hills. I told [the coach] from the beginning he better be brutal
with me because if my accent isn't perfect, *I'm going to be brutal
with him*."

The threat obviously didn't work because several critics
complained that his brogue seemed to come and go in the film.
One reviewer derisively compared his now-you-hear-it-now-
you-don't accent to Al Pacino's laughable attempt at sounding
Cuban in *Scarface*. Like Pacino, it seemed that whenever
Cruise's character got angry or had to shout, his much-practiced
brogue disappeared and his New Jersey roots slipped out in what
was supposed to be nineteenth-century Ireland and America.

For once, the actor's perfectionism failed; he flopped when
it came to impersonating an Irishman. "There comes a point,"
he said resignedly, "where you just have to forget about the
accent." That's exactly what the critics accused him of doing, as
he seesawed between a Gaelic lilt and suburban New Jersey style.

Although he competed with his wife to see who could ride
a horse faster, Cruise generously conceded the Meryl Streep
Accent Award to his wife. "Every time Nic does a movie, it
seems she has to do an accent. My hat is really off to her," he
said proudly.

"I thought it would have been a lot easier to pick up,"
Cruise said and admitted that his wife "picked it up quicker
than me" since an Australian twang is a lot closer to an Irish
brogue than Middle American is.

(When an accent didn't come easily to her, Kidman could
show herself to be as much a workaholic as her husband. In
*Billy Bathgate*, she was a rich American beauty, who was supposed to sound like a cross between Katharine Hepburn's Bryn
Mawr accent and Candice Bergen's Vassar. Kidman found this
nasal, twitty accent as hard to acquire as her husband had the
Old Sod sound. With typical perfectionism, she spent four
hours a day for three weeks with a dialogue coach trying to get
the clenched-teeth, WASP accent of the American rich down

pat. And she succeeded. While the critics loathed *Billy Bathgate*, not a single journalist saw fit to carp about an Australian actress trying to impersonate a rich American of the Roaring Twenties.)

What Cruise lacked in cost-consciousness and an ear for accents, he more than made up for in untemperamental behavior on the set. In fact, there was only one temperamental star on the set, one with four legs and a nasty bray. Displaying a rare sense of humor, Cruise described the four-legged prima donna he rode in the film. "The horse was nice, but the mule, or was it a donkey... I think they auditioned a couple of thousand donkeys to try to find *the* donkey," Cruise said. It seems that *everybody* wants to be in show business.

After a while, however, the animal began acting like a spoiled star. "The donkey started getting used to commands like 'action' and 'cut.' When the director said, 'Action,' the donkey would take off. When he said, 'Cut,' the donkey would stop on cue. As film went on, the donkey became more temperamental. When he was supposed to be moving, he just wouldn't move. I think he was holding out for more money. He was a real pain in the ass," Cruise said, flashing his multimillion-dollar grin.

While the donkey was stubborn and temperamental, as donkeys usually are, the horses in the film were downright dangerous.

Although Cruise eventually clocked his horseriding at thirty-nine miles per hour, the horses apparently were not impressed. Cruise reported that of the six times he rode the horse, the animal threw him three or four of those times. "It was the horse's fault, of course," he added, grinning again. His lack of horsemanship may be explained by the fact that the usually well-prepared actor only had five horse riding lessons before filming began, and before that he had never been on a horse. "I wanted to challenge myself," he explained with understatement.

The personable director Ron Howard and Cruise the perfectionist meshed perfectly. Unlike Don Simpson, it's a good bet that Cruise and Howard will work together again some day.

"Ron is a great director," Cruise said. "He has this ability to take all this information and keep his vision. He also saves the option to change his mind and not go absolutely crazy with details," a lesson Cruise still hasn't learned. "The man is impressive, just impressive. Ron made it easier for all of us."

Producer Grazer raved about Cruise's workaholism and how it raised the spirits of the rest of the cast and crew. Time is money on a movie set. A single day's delay, due to bad weather or a star's bad disposition, can cost $100,000 in budget overruns. It's no surprise that Grazer said admiringly, "If Tom had to go to the bathroom while we were shooting, he'd *run* to go take a pee. Not walk. *Run*. Sprint. And if Tom Cruise can run from his trailer to the set or run from the set to the bathroom, it sets the tone for everyone else. They realized how serious he was about bringing this movie in on time."

Kidman found her husband's workaholism a bit disquieting. She was accustomed to the slower pace of her native Australia, where the heat and humidity engender an almost Latin *manana* mentality.

"The American work ethic is quite frightening," she has said. "I was just amazed by the energy Americans have. That determination to succeed is rare in Australia."

And here she was, married to the hardest working man in show business. Not only was her husband's workaholism scary, it was contagious. Kidman found herself being infected with the very American Protestant ethic that work is salvation. The proof is that in recent years she has made two films to every one of her husband's. Just as the long distances in Los Angeles forced her finally to buy a car and learn how to drive, the industriousness endemic in America grabbed her and didn't let go.

*Rolling Stone* described their personalities as yin and yang. While Cruise's workaholism rubbed off on his wife, he couldn't help but be infected by her more laid-back attitude toward the brass ring of success. But in Cruise's case it was only a mild contagion. "For a long time, until I met Nicole," he admitted, "I

always put my career ahead of everything. Now we do everything together. Now work doesn't belong in the book next to
the definition 'hard, awful yoke.' It's like a whole new life
opened up. She's the most important thing to me."

Kidman may have loosened her husband up a bit, but he
never lost his trademark politeness. He described his philosophy
of on-the-set etiquette. If he ever turns it into a book a la Miss
Manners, say, *Mr. Cruise's Way to Behave on Location*, he might
include these quotes he gave an interviewer when Grazer's comments were repeated to him.

"I *never* show up late. In fact, I show up *early*. And I expect
that of other people. The crew works very hard. I understand
the importance of momentum on the set," he said.

Then echoing the courtesy he shows just about everybody,
from autograph hounds to fellow superstars, Cruise added, "It's
respectful to the director and everybody else on the set to show
up on time and do the best job you possibly can."

Besides his innate courtesy and respect for others, Cruise
may realize he's being paid a fortune to behave himself on the
set. That superstar paycheck has been defended by Grazer, the
producer. Cruise's take-home pay for *Far and Away* was $9 mil-
lion plus profit participation, and Grazer feels he earned every
penny of it. (The film didn't turn a profit, so Tom had to settle
for his upfront fee of $9 million.) "Tom is not overpaid in the
least. When you have a good movie with him, the sky's the
limit." Ironically, Grazer said that before the box-office grosses
came stumbling in.

Cruise himself was sensitive, in the middle of a recession,
about press reports oohing and aahing over his ever growing
fees. He complained to *Rolling Stone*, "The people who own
studios didn't get to where they were by being dumb business-
men. They aren't going to pay me one penny more than I'm
worth, especially in this marketplace. They wouldn't pay it if I
wasn't worth it. And the day I'm not, they won't."

Like all his predecessors, Ron Howard adored working

with Cruise. Although Howard is only a few years older than the star, once again the father figure/mentor relationship enriched the collaboration. Cruise's patented style of deferring to his seniors—be it a co-star or director—delighted Howard.

"Despite his confidence in his own ideas, Tom really wants to be directed. He wants his ideas to be edited. He's the kind of guy who won't take *yes* for an answer. He wants you to really mean it," Howard said.

Producer Grazer, however, hinted at the better known Cruise Control when he tried to put a happy gloss on the star's obsession with everything that goes into his movies. Grazer said, "Tom didn't just sit in on the marketing meetings. He *made* the meetings. He had a point of view about everything—the posters, the trailers, the distribution pattern. He's always testing you."

Then, perhaps making sure he didn't burn his bridges to some future Cruise project, Grazer hastily added, "But I don't mind it because it isn't about his ego. It's about the movie."

Cruise did indeed throw himself into the nuts and bolts of moviemaking, including doing his own stunts.

The actor had never been on a horse before outside of a pony ride during childhood, but with characteristic perfectionism, he became a master equestrian by the time filming began. He so felt the "need for speed," he even became competitive with his wife, who had grown up riding and was a far superior horseperson.

If Cruise could turn a lap at the speedway at 182 miles per hour, he wasn't about to let Mrs. Cruise beat him on the horse-trail. Kidman was clocked at thirty-five miles per hour. So, Cruise kept practicing until he hit thirty-nine miles per hour. When the timer announced Cruise's winning speed, the actor threw his fist into the air and shouted, "Yes!"

Horses at thirty-nine miles per hour are safer than cars doing 182, but Cruise's method acting approached madness once again when it came to a fight scene in the movie.

As usual, Cruise insisted on doing all his stunts. In the fight scene—which was bare-knuckled—that meant taking all the blows himself. No stunt double was called in just before the blow landed. Cruise had never boxed before—at least outside the playground—and he trained like a heavyweight contender.

"It was ferocious," he said. "I didn't realize it would be so physical. I really took a pounding. I had knuckles going into my back, my chest. And I really got hit in the ribs a lot. For about a week and a half, I was in constant pain. Once I got on my knees and just said, 'Let me have a break here, guys.' So they'd give me some oxygen and a little water, and then I'd go back to work. But boy was it brutal."

Cruise so charmed the professional boxers who beat him up on screen that whenever an unchoreographed blow landed on that $9-million body, the fighters would stop and apologize. This caused a lot of screams of "Cut!" from the normally patient director, and the scene had to be reshot, ironically adding to Cruise's pain.

Cruise's G-rated nude scene was less painful—and a lot of fun for his wife. In one scene, Cruise is asleep in a barn, totally nude except for a strategically placed chamber pot. The script called for Kidman to enter on tiptoe and lift the pot.

Ever the prude, Cruise insisted that a towel cover his loins. The camera would focus on Kidman's startled reaction, not on Cruise's crotch, so the towel wouldn't be in the way. However, the director felt that Kidman's reaction wasn't dramatic enough and finally persuaded the prudish but accommodating star to junk the towel for one take—without telling Kidman about the "costume change."

It worked. Kidman came into the barn one more time, lifted the pot, and her genuine shock was recorded on film for posterity.

Her reaction raises an interesting question. What was she shocked about? They had been married for almost two years by then. Surely she had seen what was under the pot many times before. Unless, of course, Cruise had been keeping his "instrument pure" with Kidman just as he had with Rogers.

Later, Kidman would explain away her shock by saying, "Listen, there's something very special about what's under that pot, let me assure you."

The set of *Far and Away* wasn't all fun and games and flashing. The film also marks the first time Cruise began to withdraw into himself. Normally gregarious, Cruise seemed to be turning into a classic movie star, complete with superstar arrogance and demands for special treatment.

When they weren't shooting, Cruise and Kidman retired to their sumptuous trailer, a double silver bus with a living room, microwave-equipped kitchen, queen-size bed, and a satellite dish on top. They would only come out when called to the set for a scene.

A romantic might speculate that the frisky newlyweds had better things to do than hang out at the buffet table—like trying out that queen-size bed. However, considering Cruise's alleged desire to keep his instrument spic and span, the question arises, "What exactly were they doing in that trailer all that time?"

Hiding out.

Sticking to themselves.

Evolving into Mr. and Mrs. Hughes, Greta and Greg Garbo. *Far and Away* represents the beginning of Cruise's withdrawal from public view.

Extras were ordered by an assistant director not to speak to the stars unless spoken to. When Cruise and Kidman reluctantly posed for pictures with the cast, the extras were not allowed to keep the photos. It was explained that Cruise's contract stipulated that candid shots of the superstar were not allowed. Who knows where they might turn up. An innocent arm wrapped around a youthful extra might find its way to the tabloids with a caption like, "Tom and Homosexual Lover Embrace Secretly on the Set!" Never mind that the rest of the extras, also in the

NOT FAR AND AWAY ENOUGH

shot, had been cropped out by the tab's paste-up artist. However well-intentioned, the rule about photos dampened spirits on the set. One extra lamented, "It put a real bitter taste in everyone's mouth."

Mrs. Cruise, however, was not yet ready to go the Howard Hughes/Leona Helmsley route in relating to the "little people." She managed to find time to chat up the extras and mothered the child-actors on the set.

Cruise is usually more considerate of fans, but maybe he considered the extras fellow workers who shouldn't bother a colleague under the stress of making a complicated, big-budget film.

Off duty, Cruise tends to treat fans like long lost friends. Even when fans get pushy, Gentleman Tom keeps his cool. "If people push too hard, I'll be the first one to say, 'Look, excuse me, this is not OK.' But you don't have to be a bastard about it. There are certain times when I'm out at a museum or something and I literally don't have the time so I'll say, 'How about I shake your hand because if I sign an autograph it's not fair that I don't sign everybody else's.' If they don't understand, then that's their problem. Most of the time people understand."

At least he's not as imperious as his idol, Paul Newman, who refuses fans' requests for autographs flat out. Cruise might borrow an amusing way of dealing with autograph hounds from Steve Martin. When accosted by a fan in search of his John Hancock, Martin saves times and hurt feelings by handing the supplicant a preprinted business card that says, "This is to certify that I have had a warm and meaningful encounter with Steve Martin." It's much nicer than Newman, and less voluble than Cruise's long-winded explanations at museums.

However he treated or mistreated the other workers on location, Cruise continued to treat his wife like a princess. "He was always taking care of her," one recalled. "He would put a towel around her if she looked cold, making sure she was always feeling good."

The stars managed to put even more distance between themselves and their co-workers when the film went on location in Billings, Montana, which stood in for Oklahoma during the Land Rush scenes. They junked their sumptuous trailer and moved into an even more sumptuous rented house with five bedrooms, six baths, and 7,500 square feet to luxuriate in away from the prying autograph pads of fans. Like their home in Pacific Palisades, their rented digs were totally secluded, hidden at the end of a private dirt road.

After *Far and Away* came out in 1992, it was clear the film would not be a success—at least not as big a success as previous outings. When the *Los Angeles Times*, discarding its usual fawning, nonconfrontational mode, had the temerity to ask Cruise if the box-office showing of his baby had been a disappointment, the usually affable star exploded, noting that the film had grossed $60 million in the US. Backpedalling, the gentleman from the *Times* didn't bring up the uncomfortable fact that that was $10 million short of the film's budget.

Oh well, there's always video and pay cable, and the hope, which would be fulfilled, that his next film would make amends. However, unfortunately for Universal, the next film would be made at another studio and make monster profits for somebody else.

The critics laughed at *Far and Away*. And the public stayed away.

*Far and Away* is not only significant as Cruise's second flop in a row. It also marks the beginning of Cruise Control going into overdrive.

"Control freak" is not a term Cruise believes applies to him. It's a cheap shot taken by people who don't know him, he insists. "I think people who call me a control freak haven't worked with me. I expect a lot. I have very high standards, as do the people I work with. It's not a matter of control. It's a matter of contributing to the picture."

Whatever you want to call it, his hands-on approach was aided and abetted—some say increased—by his decision to hire PMK to handle all the publicity for his films and himself.

According to many entertainment journalists, PMK is the most hated PR firm in Hollywood. It's also the most loved.

The press hates PMK. Celebrities love it. .

The West Hollywood agency represents *the* biggest names in Hollywood, from Glen Close to Demi Moore to Roseanne Arnold. This gives the agency unbelievable clout with the press, which PMK inevitably uses to club journalists over the head with.

Celebrities love PMK because most stars hate doing interviews. PMK is happy to say no to journalists and editors. After all, the agency is just earning its $1,000-plus-a-week retainer it typically charges clients.

But, according to many Hollywood journalists, PMK seems to take a sadistic pleasure in handling the press. Blithely unaware of the First Amendment, PMK's publicists are notorious for telling journalists what they can and cannot ask the stars before the interview. (Woe betide the reporter who disobeys these commandments. He or she will find himself blacklisted by PMK quicker than you can say Joe McCarthy. Any journalist who angers PMK will virtually find his career covering Hollywood over.)

Defenders of the agency might say PMK's coven of publicists are just doing their job, shielding their clients from rude journalists and those pesky, intrusive questions.

The downside to this protectiveness is that it really ticks off the press. And the only revenge the press can take against the publicists is to attack their clients. No one wants to read a hatchet job on PMK . . . but a hatchet job on Tom Cruise is irresistible.

It is no coincidence that shortly after Cruise signed on at PMK in January 1992, the first negative articles began appearing about him. He had been practicing Scientology for years, but it wasn't until PMK began representing him that the articles about his religion began to percolate in the press. The term "control freak" was first applied to him after PMK went to work for him, ostensibly to get him good press. Hiring PMK had just the opposite effect.

Former senior editor of *Los Angeles* magazine Ed Dwyer remembers his unenviable task editing a cover story about Cruise and the Church of Scientology. Pat Kingsley, the sixty-two-year-old publicist who heads PMK, bombarded him with phone calls. She even took time out from a vacation in Paris to harass him long distance. The term Dwyer used to describe Kingsley's phone etiquette was "screaming."

If Tom Cruise is a control freak, then the PR agency he hired was a perfect match for his personality.

There is some justification for Cruise's seemingly paranoid attitude toward the press. He has had some unpleasant experiences with the media, mostly in Europe.

In 1989, a London newspaper claimed he checked into a Paris hospital to take an AIDS test. His then publicist, Andrea Jaffe, explained that Cruise had gone to the hospital because he had a temperature of 104. "He was there for several days, and they ran a series of tests, which were all negative. They told him he just had a bad case of the flu. They got his temperature down, and he came home," Jaffe said.

The AIDS rumor was nothing compared to the next flight of fancy from Fleet Street. *News of the World*, a British tabloid, ran a preposterous story claiming that Cruise had breast cancer! Cruise sued and settled with the tabloid.

Unlike press control freaks such as Julia Roberts and Michelle Pfeiffer, Cruise just doesn't sweat bad publicity. "I don't compromise what I want. That's really how I live my life. If people want to be vicious because they can't say anything nice [or] because they need a story, they're the ones who have to wake up in the morning and look at themselves in the mirror. I just can't live my life by other people's standards," he has said.

If only he could communicate his *laissez-faire* attitude about the press to his press agents, the world of celebrity journalism would be a happier place. Within only a few months of signing the superstar, PMK was dictating rules to the press that had never been imposed before.

At the press junket in Los Angeles for *Far and Away*, journalists from around the world were flown in to interview the cast and director. This is standard operating procedure for a studio to promote a major release. During the two- or three-day junket, the press is wined and dined at a luxury hotel, climaxing with round-table interviews with the stars, usually five to ten reporters at each table quizzing the actors as they hop from table to table.

What was not standard operating procedure was the unique document PMK demanded all the reporters sign. If you didn't sign, you didn't get to talk to Tom and Nicole or Ron Howard. The bizarre document stipulated that the interviews generated by the junket would only be published when *Far and Away* was released and not be published anywhere except in the publications for which the reporters were accredited. PMK was demanding something that no PR firm had ever demanded before—rights to what lawyers call "intellectual property." In effect, the publicity agency, not the journalists, would own the copyright to all the reporters' hard work.

This may all seem arcane and irrelevant to the general public, which it no doubt is. But the reporters were furious, and they had a soap box from which to vent their fury—their magazines and newspapers.

The issue was so explosive—at least to the press—that the *New York Times* ran a front page story in its business section about the flap. Bernard Weinraub of the *Times*, who had the clout to refuse to sign the document, wrote the article and noted that PMK was flexing its muscles futilely since an attorney had advised him that the contract was "probably unenforcable." (A 1979 US law gives writers all rights to reprints of their articles.)

Entertainment attorney Richard Morse said flat out that the contracts "are illegal. Any type of prior restraint by contract or otherwise as far as a news-gathering and reporting agency is concerned would be considered a contract void as against public policy in that it directly contravenes not only the First Amendment but also contravenes California Constitution Article 1, Section 9, which is essentially a free speech clause."

But what's the First Amendment when you're talking about coddling movie stars?

The competition for celebrity clients among publicists is so fierce, a twenty-year veteran of the studio system said publicists are "willing to do anything to get and keep their clients happy. They will stoop to any low to suck up to their clients. I've heard about press agents picking up dry cleaning and doing grocery shopping at a client's request."

First Amendment rights are nothing compared to keeping a client happy. That seems to be the not-so-subtle message of PMK and Kidman's publicist, Nancy Seltzer, who were both behind the contract demands on the *Far and Away* junket. (Seltzer said in an interview, "I'm a strong supporter of the First Amendment, and because of that I don't wish to see it abused.")

Since the contract was unenforcable and generated so much ill will from the press, whom the studios want to keep happy for the sake of good publicity, why was it foisted on reporters in the first place?

The real aphrodisiac in Hollywood isn't beauty or even money. It's power. And the publicists who got journalists, including some from very powerful outlets like *Entertainment Tonight* and *CNN*, to sign the worthless agreements demonstrated how much power they had. *CNN* could sneak reporters into Baghdad during the Gulf War, but its editors trembled before the might of Kingsley and Seltzer.

Arnold Lipsman, Billy Crystal's press rep, and one of the more *sympatico* of them, says, "It's all about power. A lot of these publicists start thinking they're the stars. The egos in publicity are amazing. They just get off on throwing their weight around. It's a real case of the tail wagging the dog."

Even though the contracts were legal gibberish, the realization didn't stop venerable film critic Jack Matthews of *Newsday* from calling PMK's assault on the First Amendment "the final insult" and "entertainment extortion." Tom Kessler, entertainment editor for the *Dallas Morning News*, called the precedent "alarming and outrageous."

The *New York Times*'s Weinraub summed up the whole sorry business: "Movie stars expect—and are sometimes given— the same groveling treatment by journalists that North Korean leaders are accorded by the state-controlled reporters. Contrast this to the way President Bush is treated… Publicists throw their weight around, barring writers viewed as too tough."

Unfortunately for Cruise, the one bit of advice he didn't take from Paul Newman could have saved him all the bad feelings generated by PMK. Newman took his protégé aside and advised, "You have to take it easy. You have to learn what to worry about and what not to worry about. The only way you are going to survive is learning how to get thick-skinned about some things." Cruise later said, "That advice is something I think about quite often." Unfortunately, it's advice that has gone unheeded.

When Rod Lurie was writing the definitive piece on Cruise and Scientology for a cover story in *Los Angeles* magazine, Kingsley hit the roof. Lurie was already infamous for his vicious style of film reviewing, which had led one movie studio to blacklist him from its lot and advance screenings of new films.

So Kingsley had reason to fear the worst from Lurie's word processor and attempted to block him at every step, phoning from Paris and New York to provide damage control. At one point, she pretentiously told Lurie that "wars were fought over this sort of thing," referring to Cruise's right to practice his religion unmolested. Lurie shot back, "Wars were also fought over my right to print this story."

Freedom of religion lost out to freedom of the press, but not before Kingsley did her best to kill the story, including denying Lurie an interview with her client.

Cruise did respond to a request from an interview on the same subject from the much kinder magazine, *Premiere*, but he wasn't very helpful. In a letter to the magazine, he said, "It's nobody's business what my religion is."

The *Hollywood Reporter*, the industry trade paper often criticized for its cozy, non-adversarial relationship with the industry it's supposed to be covering, firmly took the side of the biggest superstar in the business and harumphed, "Imagine if a magazine article singled out the Jews in Hollywood!"

Cruise's relationship with Scientology is more significant than the spats it caused between the press and his press reps. It's even more significant than demanding a Scientology-invented sound system that cost too much be used on all his films.

For his part, Cruise categorically denied forcing anyone to join the Church or even attend classes. "I haven't asked or told anyone to do anything. If they're interested that's fine. But there's no pressure from me."

Scientology has received the kind of bad press usually reserved for Third World dictators who employ torture as diplomacy. The usually sedate *Los Angeles Times* wrote that church members are "brainwashed, alienated from society, punished for aberrant behavior, and worked like slaves." *Time* magazine did an equally withering cover story on the Church, and in a sidebar the reporter who wrote the main story detailed all the sleazy tricks he suspected the Church played on him in an effort to kill the story.

Despite its bad reputation, Cruise seems happy with his church. In his eyes, it has helped him immeasurably.

As the earnest young man confided to a shocked Barbara Walters during a post-Oscar interview in 1991, the Church "cured" his dyslexia by making him realize he never suffered from the learning disorder in the first place!

"Just recently I've found out that I'm not dyslexic. I've found a way to study that has absolutely overcome that. It's called the 'Basic Study Manual.' It was designed by [church founder and sci-fi novelist] L. Ron Hubbard. Basically it gives you a system to study with. Now I can learn quickly," Cruise told Walters.

Such a patently unscientific claim didn't go unremarked by the non-celebrity journalist crowd.

One writer who has examined Scientology suspects that the way the Church dealt with Cruise's learning disorder was to simply convince him that he wasn't dyslexic. Says the writer, who has interviewed Cruise in the past, "The Church of Scientology probably says, 'You're not dyslexic if you think you're not.'" With the same willpower that forged his billion-dollar career, Cruise perhaps put all his energy into convincing himself he was *not* dyslexic.

The executive vice president of the US National Dyslexia Foundation was enraged by Cruise's comments on the paralyzing learning disorder. Cruise seemed to be implying that dyslexia was a simple problem that could be overcome with the right mind-set—or the right religious indoctrination. Such offhandedness toward a major learning handicap had the implicit effect of saying, "Ah, it's all in your head" to someone, say, suffering from an ulcer or chronic fatigue syndrome. It heightens the devastation of the problem by placing the blame on the sufferer.

Cruise backtracked a bit when *US* magazine informed him how ticked off the dyslexia research foundation was about his "miraculous cure."

He explained, "It wasn't a matter of being cured. I was probably misdiagnosed or maybe I *am* cured!"

Dr. Kate Wachs, the clinical psychologist, believes in

"mind over matter" and that it can work what seem to be miracles. "I believe in miracles. Your mind is a very powerful tool. One of the things I do with patients who are having some [problem] is to try to teach them to overcome [the problem] by using their head. Will it to happen. It's like a self-fulfilling prophecy, only in a positive way. Nothing is impossible, including being cured of dyslexia. I believe in miracles, and I believe in God. If you think it's going to happen, it has a better chance of happening because you're willing do things that will make it happen.

"Prayer is really cognitive therapy. While praying, you're actually meditating on what you want to happen. If you have confidence and control over your life, you will take the steps to make it happen. If you don't think you can do something, you're more likely to act in a way that's counterproductive to what you want."

Cruise endows Scientology with even greater powers that could not be proved or disproved scientifically, like box-office success. He credited the Church's influence on him for his enduring popularity with moviegoers.

Cruise went on: "The negative articles about Scientology have come from an absolute point of mystery and not knowing. They talk about how this religion dictates people's lives. It's the reverse of that. It doesn't dictate anything. The whole thing is not something that's directed towards dictating. It's actually directed toward conceptual thinking and independent ideas."

The actor summed up why he is a big booster of Scientology in words that explain his adherence to such a criticized religion: "Scientology works for me. It helps me be more and do the things I want to do. Essentially Scientology has enabled me. It's just helped me to become more *me*. It gives me certain tools to utilize to be the person I want to be and personal areas I want to explore as an artist."

Lisa Goodman, the Church of Scientology's overworked press rep, came to the defense of her faith's most famous adherent. "I think it's despicable that Tom or anybody—celebrity or not—should be held up to ridicule because of their religion."

Rob Reiner, who would direct Cruise in his next film, is Jewish, and yet he also found himself singing the praises of a religion whose most famous adherent was a perfect poster boy for the faith. Reiner, who is powerful enough not to be intimidated by anybody, including Tom Cruise, volunteered without prompting, "Look, I don't know anything about Scientology, but if Scientology means you're the way Tom Cruise is, then *everyone* should be a Scientologist! He cares, and he works his butt off."

# FOURTEEN

# A Few
# Good Roles

In 1992, after two disastrous films in a row—*Days of Thunder* and *Far and Away*—an ordinary star might be, if not washed up, at least headed for a TV series—or worse, live theater! But Cruise's track record was so strong, a few ruts in the track wouldn't derail this human steam engine of studio profits.

One film executive was so terrified of alienating Cruise that he insisted he not be identified even though he was saying only nice things about the superstar. The studio executive offered this *mea culpa* for a sin he didn't feel Tom committed, called *Far and Away*. "Tom Cruise didn't bomb. The movie bombed. If someone came to me now with a Tom Cruise project *and* a good script, would I want it? You bet I would." (This was gallant but also easy for the exec to say since it wasn't his studio left holding the bag called *Far and Away*.)

An agent, also demanding anonymity, added his hosannas to all this hype. "This is a minor lull in a very strong career. *Far and Away* was too weighty for a summer movie, too ambitious, and selling it as a 'Tom Cruise picture' was a mistake by Universal."

A publicist (not Cruise's) had the harshest take on Cruise's setback, but with typical flackery, his comments weren't that harsh. "The failure of the movie reflects badly on Cruise. All of a sudden he's just another top actor." That's what Alexander Pope called "damning with faint praise."

Another studio executive volunteered this prescient comment: "One bomb won't sink him," apparently forgetting *Days of Thunder.* "If his next movie is good, they'll forget *Far and Away.*"

Who Knows? Maybe Scientology helped Cruise pick his next project.

But he probably didn't need divine intercession—or intercession by Whoever the Church's guiding deity is—to choose *A Few Good Men.* Based on the award-winning Broadway play about a few lousy men on a Marine base in Guantanamo Bay, Cuba, *A Few Good Men* probably would have been a hit for anyone lucky enough to star in the film version.

But in the case of Tom Cruise, luck had nothing to do with it. His position as the number one box-office draw in the world means that all the best scripts—and lots of turkeys—are offered to him before anyone else gets a crack at them. Cruise has so much bankability that even when he wants to do a role totally wrong for him it suddenly becomes totally right for him in the eyes of studio executives.

In fact, although Aaron Sorkin—who adapted his play for the screen—didn't, he might have written the character Cruise played with the superstar in mind. Like his "Maverick" flyboy in *Top Gun,* Cruise's Navy lawyer was haunted by the ghost of his dead father. In particular, the creepy suspicion that he would never live up to his father's expectations for him.

This is the kind of role Cruise likes to sink his psychoanalytic teeth into. One industry observer said, "Tom Cruise is the smartest guy on the face of the earth. He's found a way for the public to pay for his psychotherapy sessions by filming them . . . and make a billion bucks in the process."

It was actually his wife who found *A Few Good Men* for her husband. Kidman, who often helps him sift through scripts, has described their egoless relationship. In the world of yes-men and women, extremely successful actors and actresses often need a sounding board who will tell them the truth—not what the yes-man thinks the star wants to hear. Kidman functions as an antidote to the poisonous atmosphere of self-delusion that so many superstars seem to live in.

The script for *A Few Good Men* must have jumped out at Kidman, since the protagonist is so similar—emotionally, not professionally—to her husband. Especially the character's troubled relationship with his father.

"I like hearing Nic's notes on things. I have her read scripts. She actually saw *A Few Good Men* [on stage] and brought it to my attention. She said, 'You better find out who owns the film rights to this play because this is a role you've *got* to play.'"

After Cruise was formally offered the role, Kidman dragged her husband to the theater to see the play, and once again he was pleasantly surprised by his wife's excellent literary taste.

"She's got very good taste," he said proudly. "Hey! She married me. What can I say."

It's testament to the strength of their relationship and Kidman's self-confidence that she will say no to her husband while everyone else around him is bowing and scraping and saying, in effect, "Anything you want, Tom… "

Or as Kidman has described her less than royal treatment of the king of the box office, "We have a good working rapport. I can say to Tom, 'That sucked!' And he can say to me, 'That was terrible, do it again.' It's an ideal situation to be able to have your lover as your co-worker. You wake up next to him in the morning with a bright idea. 'Hey! Guess what?' It's conducive to making a good film."

*A Few Good Men* was comfortable, familiar Cruise terrain. He told this writer during a publicity tour for *Cocktail* that he likes characters who undergo a radical personality change by film's end. Or as one critic put it, a character who "gets religion."

In an early scene, Cruise is still playing his patented smart-ass. He's supposed to be in court, representing the Navy in some crucial case. Instead he's hitting softballs while fellow prosecutor Demi Moore begs him to get back to work. His wise-guy attitude, film fans know by now, will eventually get him his comeuppance as he turns into a charter member of the (hard)working class.

Just as his track record attracts the best scripts and directors, all the A-list stars are also hot to trot with Tom Cruise.

*Almost* all the A-list stars. Two-time Oscar winner Jodie Foster, before *Sommersby* bombed and she ended up playing second banana to Mel Gibson in *Maverick*, was offered the role of cocounsel in *A Few Good Men*. Hot off the set of *Silence of the Lambs* and her second Oscar, Foster rejected the excellent script and director because the male lead, not the female, was the focal point of the film. It was Cruise's transformation from smart ass to smart guy that propelled the plot. The female cocounsel was basically there for legal and psychological advice on coping with murderous Marines and dead fathers. In Foster's mind, the role was probably one step up from playing the protagonist's arm ornament, like a James Bond girl with brains and a law degree, but not much to do.

Demi Moore, who has starred in even more hits than Foster (although not as many prestigious ones), didn't mind playing a hood ornament with a legal degree in *A Few Good Men*. As she has in so many other underwritten roles, Moore managed to make her performance as the defense attorney who helps screw Jack Nicholson to the wall the sympathetic mother confessor to the male lead's angst.

Unlike Foster, Moore was so hot for the role she stood in line to audition for it. She also took a miserly $2-million paycheck, in contrast to Cruise's $12.5 million and Nicholson's $5 million (for fewer than two weeks' work). The studio had some leverage in knocking down Moore's fee by implying she was in competition for the role with Linda Hamilton (unlikely) and Foster (absolutely not interested). Dangling the possibility in front of her that Hamilton or Foster would gladly step into the cocounsel's shoes, Moore was haggled down to a mere $2 million. Cruise and Nicholson both hover at such Olympian heights that any game playing on the part of the studio with fees would have had the stars' reps laughing as they walked out of the meeting.

But the real A-list star *A Few Good Men* managed to attract—besides Cruise—was Jack Nicholson, *the* most respected actor in Hollywood. As the jingoistic camp commandant of the Marine base, Nicholson got to chew up the scenery for the umpteenth time. He only got paid a paltry $5 million, compared to Cruise's personal record-breaking $12.5 million, but Cruise had to be on the set for the entire shoot, whereas Nicholson earned his salary for only ten days' work. That averages out to $500,000 a day!

Cruise never brags about his wealth. Only once has he used his massive wealth to put someone down. It involved an embarrassing flaunting of his superior status aimed at a low-paid soldier, who probably deserved the put-down since he was attacking something even more sacred to a lot of men than money—masculinity.

On the set of the film, Cruise demonstrated a side of his personality that the usually self-controlled actor didn't let anyone see—at least not in public. According to *Premiere* Cruise blew up at a Marine who was moonlighting as an extra.

As the makeup man applied glop to the Marine's face, the soldier cautioned him not to make him "prettier than Tom Cruise."

Cruise overheard the crack and confronted the Marine. "What's that supposed to mean?" he snarled at the startled serviceman.

Unstarstruck, the bold GI stood up to the superstar and said, "I don't want to be a pretty boy like you."

"Yeah," Cruise shot back, "then you'd have to get a real job," referring to the Marine's low wages.

This story almost sounds apocryphal and totally out of character for the usually polite star. Maybe Cruise had heard one too many cracks about his high-pitched voice and diminutive stature. Attacking him for being too good looking may have been the last straw. Or maybe the method actor was just staying in character as the hard-driving, take-no-prisoners defense attorney he played in the film. That must have been the only time Cruise lost his temper on the set. The same Cruise Control he applies to every facet of a film project also applies to his personality.

Some would say that he would have been justified in losing his temper with co-star Demi Moore. *Variety*, which depends on the studios and stars for most of their advertising revenue, doesn't usually rock the boat or print embarrassing information unless it absolutely has to because the mainstream press has already publicized the touchy matter. But in the August 3, 1992, issue it reported that Cruise's contract stipulated that his trailer had to be closest to the set.

This particular perk didn't impact the budget, but Demi Moore's reaction to it did. *Her* contract stipulated that she could have a double trailer. The overgrown camper's size meant it had to be parked further away from the crowded set.

This did not please Ms. Moore.

She called her agent.

*Variety* reported that after "intense negotiations," Cruise was persuaded to move his trailer further away from the set—despite his contract stipulating the contrary—to allow Demi Moore to move her Winnebago-plus into his spot. This delayed shooting and cost money. (Cruise obviously had never asked for the clause in his contract in the first place since he graciously acceded to his leading lady's demand to be closest to the set, even though that perk was not in *her* contract.)

Jack Nicholson, whose agent must have had better things

to do than worry about Winnebago one-upmanship, demonstrated true superstar *noblesse oblige*. To make room for Demi's
trailer, Nicholson was required to move his camper further away
from the set as well. He didn't call his agent to complain. When
asked to move his trailer, Nicholson in his typical laid-back style
said, "Go for it."

A crew member said, "Jack couldn't have cared less. That's
just the way he is. He has more important things to worry
about than trailer placement—like his performance."

Another crew member reported that Cruise did a killer
impersonation of Nicholson, complete with all those tics like
hyperactive eyebrows and the Cheshire cat smile. And both men
already shared one obsession—with opaque sunglasses! The production assistant said of Cruise's Jack attack, "He does Nicholson better than Christian Slater," although some cynics might
say a Nicholson impression is all that Slater ever does on screen
so it's more of a performance style than an impression.

Returning to pre-*Far and Away* form, Cruise wasn't just
gracious and generous toward superstars like Nicholson. The
"little people" also found themselves charmed and overwhelmed
by the "just folks" behavior of a star who was anything but "just
folks."

Kevin Bacon, who played the prosecutor in the courtroom
drama, enjoyed a special bond with Cruise. Both men suffer
from dyslexia, even if Cruise now insists he doesn't as a result of
Scientology. Bacon, who dropped out of high school, perhaps
because of his learning disorder, spent a lot of time in Cruise's
trailer rehearsing lines.

Another Kevin on the set, Kevin Pollack, who played
Cruise's nerdy cocounsel, was also charmed by his colleague's
largesse.

Pollack remembers offhandedly admiring Cruise's pen on
the set. The next day, an identical pen was delivered to Pollack's
trailer, courtesy of Tom Cruise.

But the gesture didn't stop there. Cruise noticed that Pollack wasn't using the pen he had given him. Pollack sheepishly confessed that the pen was so expensive he was afraid to use it because he didn't want to lose it. (The pen in question was a Cartier, which retails for $175.)

Cruise didn't say anything when Pollack explained his trepidation, but a day later a production assistant knocked on Pollack's door again with yet another pen. The PA explained, "This is so you'll use the pen. If you lose it, here's another one."

Pollack later quipped, "I really enjoyed hanging out with Tom Cruise. It gave me a chance to see how the other... *one percent* lives!"

Cruise was also generous to the even "littler" people, the behind the camera drones like grips and carpenters who do all the heavy lifting and unglamorous stuff like pounding nails and fetching Demi Moore refills of Evian.

Cruise used his private jet to fly the entire cast and crew to Las Vegas for dinner and an evening of gambling. His generosity went beyond a private ferry to the gambling mecca. He rented a private salon at the ultra swank Mirage Hotel so the famous faces in front of the camera could play blackjack in privacy, away from the prying eyes and autograph books of fans.

The actor downplays his generosity and credits his mother with whatever acts of kindness he bestows on friends and co-workers. "This is who I am," he has said. "I guess we were raised to be concerned for other people. You know, my mother's Southern and a wonderful hostess, and there was always a feeling of wanting to do things for other people—whether it be cooking for the older people in the neighborhood or making sure that they got their medicine and their food. Making sure we went by to say hello to them."

As Cruise's Mother Theresa-like generosity shows, it can be good to grow up poor. Because when you finally make your fortune, you remember what poverty was like and help out others less fortunate.

"There's a positive and a negative side to having a poor

childhood," says Dr. Kate Wachs. "The positive side is that it makes you more aware of the value of a dollar. It also makes you more hardworking, more entrepreneurial, and more ingenious about how to make that dollar. If you had hardworking self-sacrificing parents who still wound up using food stamps, their hard work would communicate itself to you. The negative side of growing up poor—other than the obvious ones—is you can care too much about the value of a dollar. My mother grew up during the Depression, and her family was very poor. She would count toilet paper tissues and tell us we were using too much. If you grew up poor, as an adult you can end up anxious about money. You can't relax and enjoy those things you worked so hard for because you're still waiting for the next Great Depression. It scares the hell out of you and you feel insecure."

Obviously, Cruise only felt the positive effects of childhood poverty; his insane generosity toward friends and colleagues suggests that he doesn't feel a bit anxious about giving away a portion of his immense fortune.

Even Demi Moore was charmed by her leading man. Maybe it was the free trip to Vegas that had her gushing, "He's very smart about himself. He knows his strengths and weaknesses. He's not afraid to expose them to get what he needs."

Rob Reiner loved his accommodating star as well. "Tom is the most decent, sweetest, most wonderful person I've ever worked with," the director said.

And Kevin Pollack said, "This guy has a work ethic the like of which I've never seen. I can't believe I'm saying this, but this guy really works for his $15 million."

The camaraderie fostered by Cruise paid off in many ways. Although Cruise was the nominal star, the story really called for an ensemble cast, and Cruise generously allowed other cast members, especially Nicholson, to shine. The good feelings were evident on screen, with every performance perfectly meshing with the others.

When *A Few Good Men* was finally released in 1992, it

became the number one hit of the Christmas season, despite stiff competition from other films like *Unforgiven* and *Bram Stoker's Dracula.*

Marketing the film, however, was a nightmare for the people at the studio. First there was the matter of credits. Of course, Tom Cruise had to come first in the listing but what to do with Nicholson, a much more important actor, even if his box-office draw isn't as big as Cruise's?

After much agenting and lawyering, the crisis was solved. Cruise, Nicholson, and Moore's names would all appear on the same line (above the titles of course. Stars, at least for marketing purposes, are still more important than the movie.)

But in subtle deference to Cruise's bigger drawing power, his face in the ads would be a half inch higher than Nicholson's. And poor Demi Moore, she was low woman on this totem pole, with her head lodged another half inch below Nicholson's. The stars' agents and lawyers really earned their ten percent or $500-an-hour billing the day they organized that compromise of duelling egos.

Besides its box-office haul, *A Few Good Men* went on to collect four Oscar nominations, but curiously both director Rob Reiner and Cruise were shut out. Industry pundits speculated that Reiner and his partners at his production company, Castle Rock, were snubbed by the Academy because they had been bragging about their film in the press just a bit too much.

The public was unaware of such posturing or at least wasn't offended by it. A poll showed that *A Few Good Men* was the number one choice to win best picture, although that honor went to the vastly superior *Unforgiven* that year (1993). The disparity between public preferences and Academy voters' more elevated (but not much more elevated) tastes was underlined by the same poll's naming of Michelle Pfeiffer as their choice for best actress in the near invisible *Love Field.* (A more deserving Emma Thompson won for *Howard's End.*)

Cruise was his usual self-deprecating self, and nary a peep came from his camp about his Oscar expectations. It's more likely that the Academy was unimpressed by the cookie-cutter nature of the actor's role. Here he was again, playing a callow young man haunted by the memory of his father, undergoing a pseudo-religious experience as he matures from a wise ass to wise man in the course of two hours.

If that indeed was the Academy's reasoning, it was unfair and fallacious. Nicholson, who was nominated, was playing another character he had patented, a snarly, in-your-face iconoclast with all his trademark tics. The Academy ate up the performance and gave him the best supporting actor nod. Clint Eastwood, also nominated, didn't exactly stretch on screen either, although he did stretch behind the camera as the director of *Unforgiven*, one of the best Westerns ever made.

Once again, Cruise could console himself against the gentle contempt of the Academy for his performance by looking at his bank balance.

*A Few Good Men* grossed $350 million worldwide, even before video, cable, and network TV sales. In addition to his $12.5 million upfront fee, Cruise received a reported ten percent of the film's gross, not net. It doesn't take a calculator to figure out that even before the ancillary grosses, Cruise picked up an additional $35 million. That's more than consolation enough for getting stiffed out of a gold statuette worth about $250. (Incidentally, the figurine is gold-plated not solid gold, although its affect on a winner's asking fee is pure gold.)

# FIFTEEN

# A Firm Grip on Superstardom

Once again, Cruise's status as the top box-office draw in the world meant that all the best scripts arrived on his desk before anybody else could lay a hand on them.

*The Firm* was definitely one of the best projects in town, at least in terms of commercial potential. Based on the best-selling novel by Ole Miss-attorney-turned-pop-novelist John Grisham, *The Firm* trod familiar Cruise terrain and preoccupations.

The seemingly autobiographical elements of the storyline must have appealed to Cruise. *The Firm* is about a poor boy married to an affluent woman who feels the need to achieve financial success to compensate for his feelings of insecurity. (You can almost imagine the protagonist, Mitch McDeere, saying somewhere in a flashback in the novel the same thing the lower-middle-class Cruise promised a friend in high school: "I'm going to be a millionaire by the time I'm thirty.")

The offer that a blue-chip law firm in Memphis makes Mitch to join the team almost seems to guarantee he will accomplish that goal in the move. It offers a salary double that offered by competing law firms, country club membership, car, house—virtually the professional equivalent of winning the lottery or a gameshow.

This bonus, as in all the morality tales that so appeal to Cruise's own hyper integrity, comes with a terrible price. It's a Faustian pact that involves murder, mayhem, and the Mafia. But it's also an alliance that Cruise's hungry lawyer makes unknowingly. When he eventually discovers that his venerable law firm with its avuncular senior partners, including Gene Hackman, is a front for the mob and specializes in drug-money laundering, McDeere is terrified and unable to break away without endangering himself and his beautiful young, old-money wife.

This is the stuff bestsellers are made of... and big box-office film adaptations.

Cruise had first dibs on the project as he does with everything, "I think Tom Cruise would be perfect," Grisham, now a retired lawyer, said succinctly.

McDeere's personal odyssey is also vintage Cruise. He's even a Harvard-educated lawyer, the high school graduate's favorite alma mater on and off screen. McDeere also appealed to Cruise because the character evolves from callow youth to a responsible adult who realizes there are more important things in life than money and status.

In other words, *The Firm* was no artistic stretch for the actor. But he did want to challenge himself in another arena: directing.

Directing is the brass ring most movie stars, especially macho guys, grab for after they've grabbed every other symbol of success like Oscars and huge profit-participation percentages—not to mention double trailers on the set and other "precedential crap," to use William Goldman's term.

Tom Cruise was no exception. Many of his movie idols had already grabbed the brass ring, even though some of them found it so slippery the film slipped out of their control. Paul Newman, Cruise's mentor on *The Color of Money*, has stumbled more often than not as a director with turkeys like *Harry and Son*.

But it wasn't fear of failure that prevented Cruise from grabbing this particular brass ring. He has already demonstrated that he is virtually fearless on or off screen—whether it's skydiving with Mrs. Cruise or taking a chance on *Born on the Fourth of July*.

It was something much more typically *Cruisean* that kept him out of the director's chair and in front of *The Firm*'s cameras: his famous workaholism and perfectionism. The actor had barely taken off his Navy uniform from *A Few Good Men* when he put on Mitch McDeere's pin-striped suit. Wisely, Cruise felt he didn't have the time to prepare for his directing debut thoroughly enough.

As with so many career decisions, Cruise made the right one. He didn't let his ego, which by now has a right to be inflated but isn't, get in the way of a wise business/aesthetic decision.

Instead of hogging two hats, director and star, Cruise providentially agreed to let ultra A-list director Sydney Pollack (*Tootsie*, *The Way We Were*) take the reins. As usual, Cruise treated his elders, including the sixty-year-old Pollack, with the deference due a senior member of the industry with multiple Oscar nominations under his belt.

Pollack wasn't the only senior statesman on the set to get the full Cruise-as-idolater treatment.

Gene Hackman played his conflicted mentor on screen and apparently an unconflicted mentor between shots as well.

As he had done with much less affable co-stars like Newman and Hoffman, Cruise charmed the hell out of Hackman—so much so that when it came time to vote for the Oscar nominations, Hackman, an Academy member and two-time Oscar winner, voted for Cruise for best actor. As Hackman gushed, "He's one of the nicest people in the business." No matter how much Hackman loved Tom and his performance, once again, the Academy snubbed Cruise and nominated his older co-star, Hackman.

It's a testament to the deep affection Hackman obviously felt for his deferential co-star that he was able to slough off some obnoxious Cruise Control during marketing of the film, which would go on to gross $300 million worldwide—before cable and video, etc.

The original ad campaign for the film featured Cruise *and* Hackman's names above the title, a perk representing the stars' status and importance in putting folks in theater seats. Not only was Hackman's supporting role pivotal to the film's story and success, but he deserved above-the-title billing if for no other reason than that he was hot, hot, *hot* at the time of *The Firm*'s release. His star luster had been burnished earlier that year when he won a best supporting actor Oscar for his performance as the sadistic sheriff in *Unforgiven*.

But Cruise has a standard clause in all his film contracts that his name alone can be listed above the title. This kind of egomania is very un-Cruise-like and leads to speculation that more "precedential" agenting is at work here. (Especially when you realize that the clause has even kept Nicole Kidman's name off that precious perch above the title!)

To the public at large, this jockeying for position on a movie poster and newspaper ads seems like the stuff of lunacy. But in the movie industry, a business based on enough power symbolism to keep graduate-student semioticians in doctoral dissertations for years, perception is everything.

Having his/her name above the title solo attests to the star's drawing power, since the name is the first thing the moviegoer sees, presumably. It also means the star is implicitly more important than the film itself, since the name supersedes the title.

The supremely egoless Gene Hackman, one of the few older stars who hasn't gotten cranky with age, doesn't care about precedential treatment. By rights, the senior actor could have put up a stink, but he didn't.

He did get a little revenge against the studio, however. He had his name taken off the credits altogether, denying Paramount a crucial marketing tool—the name of an Oscar-winning actor who could help Cruise put even more people in theaters, especially older people who would be lured there by the star of *The French Connection.*

Despite the post-production battle of egos and star-billing, the set of *The Firm* was a happy one, with Cruise showering his latest mentor, Hackman, with praise and questions about their craft.

There were no prima donnas to spice things up. Jeanne Tripplehorn, who played the homicidal lesbian in *Basic Instinct,* played Cruise's patrician wife. Her star status wasn't lustrous enough for her to make demands like double trailers and inches-long commuting distance to the set. And Hackman, like other superstars of his generation, such as Jack Nicholson, didn't ask for star treatment either.

Cruise was paid $15 million for *The Firm* up front, plus his usual ten percent of the gross. After foreign, video, and TV/cable sales, his take-home pay would near $45 million. That's the same amount Jack Nicholson got for grinning his way through *Batman.* The studio wasn't carping about Cruise's haul because the huge amount still wasn't anywhere near the lion's share of the $300 million that enriched Paramount's stockholders.

Even the phenomenal success of *The Firm* may have seemed ho-hum to Cruise at this point—another day, another blockbuster. But in March of 1993, Cruise decided to try something new. He finally got to get behind the camera and direct a project.

It was a small, modest project, only thirty minutes long. Cruise's directing debut was something called "Frightening Frammis," a segment of the Showtime cable channel's *Fallen Angels* series.

Cable is the preferred place where superstars in front of the camera often decide to make their directing debut. It is a way of hedging your bets and not embarrassing yourself too widely if your debut isn't too hot.

But Cruise's maiden directing effort was far from an embarrassment. In fact, it was the best episode in a series that employed other actors-turned-director like Tom Hanks.

Cruise's "Frightening Frammis" was a dead-on homage to the 1940's film-noir style, complete with a *femme* who was lethally *fatale*. Unlike Hanks's entry, there were no self-conscious camera angles or other typical first-time director business like excessive zooms or a cameo appearance by the star-turned-director. (For his directing debut on an episode of *Fallen Angels*, Hanks apparently was so jealous of his stars, he gave himself a cameo as a TV repairman who gets electrocuted when an angry customer shoves his head through the TV tube. The rest of the cast was not famous, and the sudden appearance of a superstar in the film ruined the illusion that these were ordinary people in extraordinary circumstances.) His stylish direction was so professional and unamateurish, if his name hadn't been on the credits, you would not have known there was a novice, albeit a famous one, behind the camera.

It will be interesting to see if Cruise one day does a "Robert Redford" and decides to direct a small feature film for his big-screen debut. Redford swept the Oscars with his debut, *Ordinary People* in 1981.

If his Showtime effort is any prediction of future accomplishments, Cruise should forgo his zillion-dollar paycheck and make a similar, small-scale film, then roll a shopping cart up to the podium on Oscar night.

If he needs help from established directors, he can always call on men like Rob Reiner and Sydney Pollack, who adore him. He could probably even get some of his other "fans," like Hoffman and Hackman, to work on his feature-film debut... for scale.

# SIXTEEN

# Fangs a Lot, Fans

It was not the kind of reception the Star of the Decade was accustomed to. An angry mob had gathered outside Crossroads Market & Bookstore in Houston. The estimated thousand-plus picketers held signs that echoed their chants: "No, Tom Cruise! No, Tom Cruise!"

What had Cruise, *People* magazine's Sexiest Man Alive, the highest paid, most popular actor in Hollywood at $15 million plus per picture, done to elicit the fury of the mob?

In July 1993, the thirty-one-year-old actor had agreed to star in *Interview with the Vampire*, the first of four novels by Anne Rice about a vampire named Lestat. Lestat would be the first villain, albeit a sympathetic one, Cruise had ever played. It would also be a big departure from the patented guy-next-door stud his fans had to date paid $1.6 billion to see on the big screen.

Lestat is an ugly customer, no garden variety bloodsucker, he. When this ghoul gets lonely, he bites a victim and turns him or her into a fellow member of the living dead. Feeling paternal, he sinks his teeth into a seven-year-old girl, which freezes her at that age forever. When he falls in love with the grown woman in a seven-year-old body, it looks pretty much like pedophilia. And if a victim doesn't turn him on, he drains *all* the poor wretch's blood and leaves him for dead.

As one critic pointed out, in today's terms Lestat would be considered a serial murderer. And in modern sensibilities which have been sensitized to sexual abuse by the McMartin case and the accusations against Michael Jackson, Lestat is a child molester.

So Tom Cruise, after successfully specializing in cads who undergo dramatic transformations into decent human beings, was suddenly starring as a serial-murdering child molester!

While some might praise Cruise for attempting such a controversial role so unlike his previous all-American film outings, the mob outside Crossroads was in no mood to praise an actor who wanted to stretch. Besides, the protesters weren't fans of Cruise enraged that their golden boy was going to play such a creepy-crawly character. They didn't want Cruise to play *their* vampire. For although Lestat sounds like a synergistic cross between Ted Bundy and Jeffrey Dahmer, the ghoul with a serious overbite has his own fan club. Or more accurately, there's a fan club for the four novels which chronicled Lestat's life of involuntary blood donations. These cultists, whose fervor resembles that of Trekkies, felt Cruise was dead wrong for the role and had turned out *en masse* to make their displeasure known.

Fortunately, Cruise was nowhere near this mob scene—not even in the state of Texas.

The crowd had ostensibly assembled to welcome Anne Rice, in town to promote her new novel, *Lasher*. As the squat, raven-haired novelist emerged from her limousine, a fan approached and handed her a petition with hundreds of signatures.

What was the angry group demanding?

A boycott of the film version of their beloved novel, *Interview with the Vampire*.

Rice would not have any qualms about acceding to this demand since she was the instigator and chief cheerleader for the anti-Cruise sentiment. In interviews that circulated all over the world, Rice poured gasoline on her fans' fiery contempt for the casting of an archetypal nice guy as an archetypal fiend.

"Cruise is no more Lestat than Edward G. Robinson is Rhett Butler," she said. Rice had publicly lobbied for Daniel Day-Lewis, Jeremy Irons, or John Malkovitch, all experienced at playing Euroristocrats. Day-Lewis, who unquestionably could have turned in a *tour de force* performance as Lestat, had turned down the role because he was tired of playing Eurotrash in costume dramas. Irons and Malkovitch, both exceedingly talented actors, weren't considered big enough names for a $50-million extravaganza.

The film's director, Neil Jordan, claims Cruise was his personal choice, though even if he wasn't, the director didn't have the kind of clout to nix a superstar of Cruise's caliber anyway.

Jordan chided Rice for suggesting Malkovitch or Irons, saying her choices were too predictable. He didn't want the clichéd vampire look with cadaverous faces and sunken eyes, features both Irons and Malkovitch would have been able to do on screen with a minimum of makeup in contrast to the full-faced Cruise.

"Sometimes when you go the opposite way from what people expect, you get the best results," Jordan said. And Cruise was about as opposite as the fans of the Rice books could expect (short of Clint Eastwood doing a transvestite turn in *La Cages aux Folles III*). "Every casting choice is a leap. And if it works, it's because the actor makes it fit his own skin," Jordan said.

When Cruise expressed interest in the project, Warner Brothers executives leapt for joy. They fell all over themselves to sign up the hottest box-office star since Clark Gable.

In Rice's richly detailed saga, which has achieved cult-status since it was published nearly two decades ago, Lestat is an eighteenth-century French nobleman: blonde, gorgeous, and a strapping 6'2". Cruise claims to be 5'9", although he looks a lot closer to 5'7" in person. He has dark brown hair, and his preppie good looks, invaluable for a matinée idol, don't conjure up images of decadent eighteenth-century aristocracy.

When Cruise signed on to play Lestat in July 1993, the brickbats started almost immediately. Julia Phillips, the producer who had been fired from the project after she badmouthed executive producer David Geffen in her sulfurous memoir, *You'll Never Eat Lunch in This Town Again*, imagined Tom Cruise portraying the role. Phillips raised her gravelly alto to a falsetto Minnie Mouse pitch and impersonated Cruise announcing, "I am the Vampire Lestat."

Nicole Kidman came to her husband's defense and dismissed Rice, Phillips et al. with her typical *sang froid*: "Well, great. Now let's see what he's going to do with it. You know it just says that they're all narrow-minded. I know he's going to be great in the movie. Honestly, Anne Rice doesn't understand actors. People who say that do not understand actors."

Pundits quickly labeled the film "Cruise's Coffin," and "Geffen's Grave." Others suggested "Fangs a Lot" for screwing up the casting of a much loved book.

Geffen felt compelled to speak out, something this Howard Hughes of movie moguls almost never does. Rice's criticism, he said, "lacks kindness and professionalism"—not to mention gratitude; the billionaire producer had paid her a record $2 million for movie rights to her four vampire novels: *Interview, The Vampire Lestat, Queen of the Damned* and *Tales of the Body Thief.*

Geffen also speculated that her objections to Cruise were a publicity stunt to promote her new novel. In a show of pique, Cruise himself decried all these objections to a film that hadn't even been shot yet. "When it first hit, it really hurt my feelings to be candid about it," he said. "I just couldn't resist the role."

Cruise wouldn't stoop to mud-slinging attacks on his critics except to say "their *venom* really hurt. I found it personally hurtful. But I can't do anything about that; I've just got to play the character."

Then the actor offered a revisionist interpretation of Lestat's wicked character, which must have seemed like garlic and crucifixes to devotees of the Rice books. Lestat's "not a bad guy," Cruise announced. "He just has villainous aspects to him. From his point of view, he's right. He's really a terribly lonely character."

Rice fans were already having nightmares that the monstrous Lestat would be transformed into basically a nice guy with an unfortunate addiction to hemoglobin. The only thing missing from Cruise's published comments about his role, Rice fans felt, was an addendum that in the film version Lestat would also be an ace volleyball player and a hot air balloon aviator in eighteenth-century France!

For her part, Rice couldn't get the reclusive David Geffen on the phone, so she announced in public what he didn't care to hear in private. Rice said, "I wanted to call David Geffen and say, 'How the hell could you do this?'"

His response, if he had deigned to return her call, might have been what everybody in Hollywood knows. Tom Cruise's name on a marquee almost guarantees that a movie, no matter how icky, will turn a profit. It's called bankability, and Cruise is *the* most bankable star in Hollywood.

Whatever Rice's real motivation was for berating Cruise, the brouhaha did succeed in generating a lot of publicity, as the mob outside the Houston bookstore proved.

Or, as Warner Brothers's publicity chief Rob Friedman said, "It's no coincidence that *Interview* is back on the bestseller list after seventeen years. It's just good old-fashioned hucksterism."

Casting decisions usually don't generate this kind of publicity or venom. Certainly they don't create pickets unless ethnic issues are involved. Native Americans are outraged when WASPs get juicy Indian roles. When white stunt doubles painted their faces black to impersonate African-American stars, the NAACP went through the roof. But all this anger over an eighteenth-century Frenchman, and an imaginary one to boot?! We're not talking about hiring Danny De Vito to play Lincoln or Madonna to play Eleanor Roosevelt.

Tom Cruise's desire to play Lestat wasn't as crazy as it sounded. The versatile actor did have a successful track record in challenging roles. "I just had to do it," he said, explaining why he decided to tackle such a difficult, unpleasant role.

It wouldn't be the first time Cruise had felt the need to step outside his good-guy, good-looking pigeonhole. The last time he stretched, as a balding, paraplegic vet named Ron Kovic, in *Born on the Fourth of July*, he won his first and only Oscar nomination. He had proved he could prosper outside the volleyball and law courts. But the cult-like fans of the vampire novels didn't want him stretching on "their" turf.

The anger of the mob was just further proof of the intense feelings America's number one star engenders no matter what he does, whether it's divorcing a wife or playing a creepy nightcrawler with a yen for little girls and lots of plasma.

And just as he compensated for his smallish frame by pumping iron religiously when the role called for a buffed bod, Cruise threw himself into the role of the eighteenth-century aristocrat-turned-vampire. Or as he described his historical research on the period, "I busted ass."

He visited Versailles, home of France's dethroned kings, to soak up the feel of the gilded life of a long-vanished culture of excess. His research had him haunting museums all over the City of Light for an insight into the darkness of Lestat's soul.

His method-actor mania led him to a reversal of his pre-production regimen for athletic films like *Top Gun* and *All the Right Moves*. Instead of torturing his baby fat into muscle as he had for those projects, Cruise dropped twelve pounds after some ferocious dieting, all in service of the role, which required a gaunt look for the protagonist. Supremely unvain, he sports stringy dirty hair in the film, which he allowed to be flecked with gold, along with his eyebrows.

When shooting began in New Orleans, where much of the three-centuries-spanning saga takes place, the set was not surprisingly closed to all outsiders, especially the press.

The TV tabloid show *Hard Copy* was not deterred and paid handsomely for a videotape that was shot with a zoom lens.

What a shock!

The grainy, out-of-focus footage revealed a totally unrecognizable Cruise, with a gold-flecked fright wig and a complexion that looked as though it was being consumed by the killer Strep A bacteria. The least narcissistic matinée idol on the planet—except when the role calls for a body beautiful, which he then shows off to the fullest—Cruise as Lestat had apparently been caught in the sunlight; his face had become a network of tiny burst blood vessels that looked more like tertiary syphilis than a vampire who was photo-sensitive.

Anne Rice and her partisans could have saved their breath and their venom complaining over the casting of Cruise. He was so unrecognizable that the studio could have saved itself some money and cast Jon Lovitz as Lestat and filmgoers would have been none the wiser.

The complaints about his diminutive stature also became irrelevant when the videotape revealed that he was the same height as co-star Brad Pitt, the washboard-abbed actor who plays his sometime lover, the tragic Louis. Pitt, who *is* a strapping six-footer, was eye-to-eye with his 5'7" co-star, who had obviously grown several inches through the low-tech movie magic of high heels or a soap box. (The video didn't show his feet.)

By the time shooting began, the miscasting was old news, but Cruise himself is always news, so the press had to come up with another angle to write about. Even reputable publications got in on all the scandal-mongering, sometimes with questionable results.

*New York* magazine, the same publication that earlier claimed Cruise's publicist rejected fifteen *Rolling Stone* reporters before settling on a pushover journalist, printed an item claiming Cruise had demanded and got a secret underground passageway built from his trailer to the set so he wouldn't be bothered by fans.

Pat Kingsley was for once helpful to the press and explained that the "tunnel" was actually an above-ground canvas tent to shield him from paparazzi and keep Lestat's grotesque physiognomy a secret until the film came out at Christmas in 1994.

Whether it was a tunnel or a tent, there's no such thing as opaque when the paparazzi want a story, as the *Hard Copy* video, which aired endlessly on the show, proved. Rather than hiding his gruesome visage, it's entirely likely that what Cruise really didn't want leaked to the press was what he was doing in the video footage.

Kissing Brad Pitt!

Perhaps Cruise wanted to spare his heterosexual fans a heart attack until absolutely necessary, when the films opened.

A more vicious rumor, reported by the usually scandalphobic *Los Angeles Times*, was that Cruise had demanded that all homoerotic elements between him and his studly co-star Pitt be expunged from the script. As the secret videotape showed, that rumor was genuine fiction.

The director also came to Cruise's defense and said, "After directing *The Crying Game*, do you think I would let *anybody* tone down the homoeroticism in this film? To accuse me of taking all the homoerotic elements out of the movie—after I made *The Crying Game* . . . ! Me of all people! Why would I do that?!"

He makes a good point, although it misses an even bigger one: if Cruise had wanted the homosexual subtext obliterated, all the erotic hanky-panky would have been gone faster than you can hit the DELETE button on your word processor.

It's testament to Cruise's courage and his rumors-be-damned attitude that he didn't tamper with the script, at least not the homoerotic elements. It's a good bet that he did tear apart the rest of the script as he has done on every project since *Top Gun*, when he diluted its jingoism with apolitical macho camaraderie.

One Hollywood authority says, "Cruise never met a script he didn't like... so much so that he felt he had to put his imprint on it. It may drive writers batty, but his tampering inevitably improves the final product. *Top Gun* might have elicited the fury of the liberal press, which attacked the anti-Communist flavor of *Rambo* and made Stallone a laughingstock among the more sophisticated reviewers. A lot of critics still hated *Top Gun* for being mindless entertainment, but at least their reviews didn't have the kind of venom they reserve for mindless films that are also politically incorrect.

"Cruise is a member of that dreadful celebrity fraternity called limousine liberals. But in the case of *Top Gun* that kind of superficial lipservice to liberalism that these celebrities pay resulted in a film that didn't have liberals in the audience cringing the way they did when Stallone grunted his political philosophy in *Rambo*.

"It's amazing, but even his politics help him make more money. If *Top Gun* had been as jingoistic as *Rambo*, it probably would have made a $100 million less than what it did. Cruise doesn't just have a golden gut, he's got a golden touch. Whatever he touches, massages, and reworks, no matter how drecky it is to begin with, ends up a monster blockbuster.

"If he ever really wants to stretch, he should become the head of a movie studio. Such a position would be his for the asking. The studio's parent company, like Sony, would kick out the head of production at Columbia tomorrow—no, this afternoon—if Tom Cruise wanted the job.

"But he wouldn't take it. He's having too much fun, the time of his life, starring in one hit after another. Maybe when he's old and ugly he'll become a 'suit,' but that won't be for decades. If Sean Connery can play a bald, sixty-something leading man when he should be collecting Social Security, you can bet your reservation at Morton's that Cruise will be playing sexy octagenarians when he hits his eighties. He'll cast Nicole as Grandma Moses in one film and himself in *Cary Grant: the Golden Years*. Then he can star in *The George Burns Story* and *Uncle Miltie Goes to Town*. He'll be sending studio execs notes from his grave!"

The film's executive producer David Geffen, who only recently came out of the closet as the first openly gay movie bigwig at an AIDS fundraiser, verified that Cruise employed a hands-off policy toward the homoeroticism in the script.

Said Geffen, "Tom has not had any input into this script whatsoever. There's not one iota of truth in it. Any homophobia being alleged against Tom is an outrage and a bald-faced lie."

Still desperate for a story after exhausting the Rice and homoerotic angles, one magazine headlined a piece about the film as "Tom's Big Gamble," suggesting that the film could make or break him. But after his two mega-hits *A Few Good Men* and *The Firm*, even if the film did flop, his reputation probably wouldn't suffer much. Nothing at this point in his billion-dollar career could break Tom Cruise.

But now, all such speculation is moot. As it turned out, fans gave *Interview with a Vampire* their ultimate seal of approval; they turned out in hordes at the theaters. The film grossed $150 million—a far cry from the disasters some projected.

Even Rice herself, after all that ranting and raving, had to admit in the end that Cruise nailed Lestat's character with fiendish perfection. In fact, she took out a full-page ad to publicly apologize for her earlier biting remarks and went on record as being "pleasantly surprised" with Tom's ghoulish performance.

Apparently the critics were pleased as well. *Interview* won solid reviews on almost every front. As for Cruise, he enjoyed his transformation from babe to beast so much he said he might even give us another round. *Interview*, he said, is the "only film I would ever consider doing a sequel to."

That one statement, however, doesn't mean it's going to happen. Cruise is one of the only superstars who hasn't starred in a sequel—and for good reason. Sequels are typically the hallmark of a fading career. And Cruise's career is hardly sliding, especially after the double home run of *The Firm* and *Interview with the Vampire*. Superstars tend to make sequels after a few embarrassing flops. For years, Sylvester Stallone kept his star burnished by appearing in seemingly endless visitations to Rocky and Ramboland. All his original efforts failed until just recently when those like *Cliffhanger* and *Demolition Man* showed he could make money without Roman numerals attached to a film title. Eddie Murphy's *Beverly Hills Cop III* was also seen as a desperation move (and one that didn't pay off).

Tom Cruise doesn't make sequels because he doesn't have to. There's a certain artistic integrity and nobility in saying no to the movie disease of sequelitis. Steven Spielberg has steadfastly refused to make sequels to any of his films, except for *Raiders of the Lost Ark*, and in that case, his reluctant willingness was due to a promise he made to the film's producer, his best friend George Lucas, to make two sequels if the first *Raiders* flew. It did, and he did. But his otherwise strict policy against sequels explains why there's never been an *ET—The Return*. And all the speculation about Spielberg making *Jurassic Park II* will probably remain just that—speculation.

"Tom Cruise is just not a sequel kind of guy," says Liz Smith, gossip columnist for New York *Newsday*. Now that Cruise has beat the odds and earned grudging praise for tackling Lestat in *Interview with the Vampire*, sequel talk is in the air again. Besides the certain windfall, a sequel makes sense since there are four more bestselling novels about Lestat just waiting to be made.

But Cruise's publicist, Pat Kingsley, quickly nailed the coffin shut on talk about a sequel to the Lestat saga. Though Cruise has said it's possible, nothing is certain, or even probable. "Unless the script is extraordinary, it's unlikely Tom would be tempted back," Kingsley said. "It was the very superior quality of the original material that attracted him in the first place. But of course he hasn't seen a script yet for a vampire sequel so let's not hazard a guess. Anything is possible.

"After all, who could have imagined he'd play Lestat to begin with?"

# SEVENTEEN

# Casa Cruise-Kidman

In February 1993, the Cruises adopted a baby girl, born a month earlier, whom they named Isabella Kidman Cruise.

The Cruise adoption, like just about everything else he does, generated unnecessary controversy.

Isabella's birth mother, who put the infant up for adoption through a private baby broker, didn't know the identity of the adoptive parents. And Isabella's new mom and dad wanted to keep it that way. Tom and Nicole didn't want the biological mother finding out that her daughter had new parents worth roughly half a billion dollars and suddenly have a change of mind and want her baby back—or in lieu of that, receive a nice cash consolation prize.

It has happened before.

To avoid a costly blackmail scheme, although there was no indication such a scheme was in the offing by the birth mother, the Cruises tried to stop the Australian magazine *New Idea* from printing photos of baby Isabella. They went so far as to seek a court injunction against the magazine for violating Australia's law of confidentiality.

The Australian press is only slightly less clamorous than their US counterparts, and the judge denied the Cruises' injunction.

There was some Cruise Control operating here, verging as it occasionally does on paranoia. Cruise's stated reason for seeking the injunction against the baby photos was to prevent the birth mother from identifying her child and thus finding out who the baby's illustrious adoptive parents were. But it's very unlikely that the biological mother could have identified the baby, which was several months older than she was at adoption.

Four months later, on an apparently slow news day, the American press swarmed all over Cruise and Kidman when they showed up at the West Palm Beach, Florida, courthouse. The press got the story wrong, claiming the Cruises were adopting a second daughter. As it turned out, they were simply back in court to finalize the adoption of their one and *only* child at the time.

Florida law requires that you appear in court with the child, which Tom and Nicole reluctantly did. After a ten-minute court proceeding, they emerged to the blinding glare of paparazzi flashbulbs. Not wanting a repeat of the Australian photo mess, Cruise covered his daughter's face and pleaded with the unmoved photographers, "Leave us alone, will you please?"

The Cruises' second child, Connor Antony Kidman was born a whopping eight pounds on February 6, 1995. The couple adopted the baby two weeks later. The adoption took place in the same state, Florida, where two years earlier they had adopted their first child.

Florida has adoptive-friendly laws, unlike California, which explains why they flew across the country to pick up both their bundles of joy.

In fact, Florida's adoption laws are so easily manipulated that a Republican gubernatorial candidate, Anthony Martin, called for an investigation into the Cruise adoptions, calling them egregious examples of "baby-selling."

When Cruise made some nasty public comments about the candidate in return, the politician shot back with a $50-million lawsuit against the actor for defamation.

The adoptions also stirred up problems of a different kind. The fact that the Cruises adopted instead of having their own children is just one more reason for Hollywood (and other) gossips to raise their eyebrows. The couple, however, doesn't feel they owe any explanations. When a writer from *Vanity Fair* tried to coax information out of Nicole Kidman by suggesting that fans might be curious about the adoptions, she replied coyly, "They can continue to wonder." However, the superstar did reveal a little, saying, "I would like to give birth to two children. I would like to experience that. But if I don't, it's not going to destroy me."

An unfortunate irony arises out of this chapter of Cruise's life. It seems the more he and his wife try to protect their privacy and refuse to answer the public's prying, personal questions, the more intriguing and mysterious they appear. Fans become more engrossed and seek out the intimate details of their lives with new energy. Rumors abound.

The speculation surrounding the absence of biological children in the Cruise household is no exception to this rule. The Cruises' decision to adopt, along with Mimi Roger's comments regarding her ex-husband's sexual practices in *Playboy*, Cruise's curious abstinence from sex during high school, and his later rejection of willing, in fact eager, groupies all keep the public wondering about his sex life, or lack thereof.

But the speculation goes even further than that. What really goes on behind the closed gates of Cruise's estate is a constant topic of conversation among his most curious fans and the media.

Perhaps because of the intense fascination the adoring public has with their movie stars fired by the ever-greedy lust for a juicy story, rumors regarding Cruise's sexuality have been popping up and ballooning ever since he hit it big.

This is a topic at least one of the Cruises felt moved to comment on. In a gust of anger, Nicole Kidman hotly denied in *Vanity Fair* all rumors that she or her husband are gay. "I did not marry into a marriage of convenience. I would never, ever do that," she said firmly. "You marry for love. We're both heterosexual. We have a lot of homosexual friends, and neither of us would shy away from having a homosexual role. He played the vampire Lestat and didn't give a shit. But I take offense if people say I would marry into a marriage of convenience. I think that's very sexist, because they're saying, 'She married for fame and money.' It's bullshit."

As for Tom being a closeted homosexual, Kidman is willing to put her money where her mouth is. "I'll bet all my money I've ever made, plus his, that he doesn't have a mistress, that he doesn't have a gay lover, that he doesn't have a gay life," she snapped.

So where do all the rumors come from? Why do so many people still believe he's gay? Nicole's answer tells us what we've known from the beginning, "He's mighty fine-looking, and he's worth having a fantasy about."

The circumstances surrounding the adoptions of the children may not have been ideal, but the Cruise family life ever since seems to make up for it. These superstars are hands-on parents. Paparazzi have documented them strolling in Central Park with baby in tow. On her syndicated talk show, host Leeza Gibbons commented that she once saw the Cruises *en famille*, "and I was touched at how loving they were toward their two kids. They really are hands-on parents."

When his wife was filming in Toronto a year ago, Cruise accompanied her to the location. While there, he enrolled his daughter Isabella in a "Parent-Tot" gymnastic program.

Another parent in the class remarked on how un-starlike the superstar was in class. "He participated with great enthusiasm as we did the Hokey Pokey dance and sang Barney songs with our children. He truly is unaffected, and his normality was not what us common folk would expect from a big star," the woman said.

Pop psychologists say you either raise your children exactly the way you were raised or completely differently, depending on your evaluation of your childhood, whether it was happy or not.

Like so much of pop psychology, this theory is absurdly reductionist. Except for victims of child abuse, most childhoods are a combination of ups and downs, good times and bad.

Cruise's early years certainly combined the best and worst of times.

On the debit side, there was his father's financial abandonment of the family, preceded by an emotional abandonment when dad was still on the premises.

On the positive side, Cruise grew up as the only male child, adored by his sisters and encouraged in all his endeavors by a mother who loved unconditionally.

In interviews, the actor hints that he will raise his children with the best elements of his own upbringing, while making sure that unlike his own father he remains a hands-on dad to Isabella and Antony.

Four years before adopting Isabella, Cruise was already contemplating life as a responsible parent. As he micromanages every other aspect of his career and personal life, it's not surprising that fatherhood even four years in the future was something he planned to manage in a well thought out way.

"I've never had children before. I don't know what it's going to be like. But this is something my wife and I talk about, what we went through in growing up. We don't want our kids to grow up that way."

Cruise was evidently still conflicted about his childhood because in the next breath he contradicted his wish for his children to grow up differently.

"We want to set a certain standard: 'Look, you make your bed, you clean your room; that's your responsibility.' The same way we were raised. Just giving them a responsibility: 'If you do this, you get this.' A sense of accomplishment. The kids aren't going to turn sixteen and immediately get a car. Of course, I'm saying that now. I hope I won't do that."

In a few paragraphs, Cruise managed to contradict his beliefs about child rearing three times.

It is hard to imagine the insanely generous actor, who gives zillionaire producers like Don Simpson $25,000 tuition to race-car school, denying his own children a car for their sixteenth birthday. The parking lot at Beverly Hills High, the real life inspiration for *Beverly Hills 90210*, is filled with late model Porsches and Corvettes. Cruise will probably send his kids to private schools rather than a public one like Beverly Hills High, but the parking lot there will still have the same kind of cars. It will be hard for him to resist his kids' auto envy in the face of so much peer pressure.

Without having any children at the time, the generous future dad was already hoping he wouldn't resist his children's request for wheels.

*"Of course, I'm saying that now...I hope I won't do that."* So far it seems Cruise is a pretty indulgent parent. While his wife was rehearsing for her appearance as host of *Saturday Night Live,* he took his sister Lee Anne and Isabella to the Big Apple Circus.

Isabella was not amused. Early on, she began screaming and crying. Cruise unsuccessfully tried to quiet his charge, failed, and left the circus. Ever the doting parent, he planned to return the next day, hoping Isabella would take more kindly to the elephants the second time around. But his wife got a break from her TV rehearsals, and they decided to hit Central Park instead.

Cruise is so concerned about his children's future he actually lived in the Brazilian rain forest for a time to see close up the destruction of their future source of oxygen. He went to Brazil as a representative of the Earth Communications Office or ECO, an environmental group which has a huge roster of celebrity supporters, including Ted Danson and Whoopi Goldberg.

Many celebrities glom onto a popular but not controversial cause like the rain forests or ocean pollution because it's a win-win situation. Come out for gay rights, and people will suspect you have an ulterior motive. Push for abortion rights, and Pro-Lifers may chain themselves to the gates of your estate. For the same reasons, celebs will flock to fundraisers for *pediatric* AIDS charities, but stay away from similar galas for the adult victims of AIDS because of the homosexual stigma attached to the disease.

But no one is pro-pollution of the ocean. And no one except Brazilian loggers is in favor of denuding the rain forest.

Still, Cruise hasn't focused on a trendy cause because it's safe and non-controversial. He is genuinely worried about the air his babies will breathe when they grow up.

"I want to understand it more," he said in explaining his trip to the rain forest. "I want to see it. I want to make sure that there's going to be air to breath when my children are my age. It's one of the most important issues that this world has to face right now."

Cruise didn't need to read Dr. Spock's baby books for a guide to bringing up his children. His mother's example is textbook enough for him on the right way to raise a socially responsible child. Cruise likes to quote his mother a lot.

"I learned from my mother that there was opportunity in life, that you could do anything you wanted. My mother also taught us decency and respect for other people. It's like, you see some guy throw a little piece of paper out the window when you're driving—that pisses me off.

"My mother taught us that you don't do stuff like that. If you work hard, you get paid for it. That's what you do. And you do it better than anybody else has done."

Having children in his life has brought back memories of his father as well; they have been an epiphany for Cruise. For

years, he felt his father, who abandoned the family after divorcing his mother, never cared for him. They had a tense reunion
just before the older man died in 1984. But looking at his children, he says, makes him realize his father had to have loved
him, despite his seeming indifference.

Cruise has said, "You know, I loved my father very much. I
think sometimes what it would have been like for him to see me
with my daughter. When I look at Isabella, I realize that there is
no possible way that a parent can't love their child."

Cruise and Kidman have found a refuge away from the big
city and its enquiring minds and photo ops in tiny Telluride,
Colorado, although controversy has still followed them to this
sleepy hideaway of the rich who wish they weren't so famous.

When Cruise purchased a parcel of property, it was reported in the press that he had levelled a pristine valley to create a
football field!

Cruise is a generous supporter of all sorts of ecological
causes, and the rumor that he had raped the countryside sent
him into overdrive. In a public statement, he explained that he
had merely "landscaped the valley" on his property. "Every spec-
ification of the Cruise house and grounds has been done
through the auspices of environmental groups. For every tree
cut down another has been planted," he said.

Cruise was even more politically correct about another
touchy subject: hunting. The previous owner of his property
had allowed hunters to bag the elk that like to migrate across
the property. Cruise, through his publicist, announced, "Hunting will no longer be allowed there."

Late last year, Cruise was embroiled in more controversy,
this time of his own doing. He sued Philips Interactive Media of
America for $10 million, accusing the company of using footage
from *Top Gun* without his permission in a commercial for its
Magnavox video recorder.

Cruise certainly doesn't need the money, but the suit is
indicative of his hands-on approach to everything that touches

his life, whether it's doing the hokey-pokey with his daughter at gym class or protecting the use of his very public image. It's clear that he is as protective of his image as Disney is of Mickey Mouse's.

Cruise is simply a hands-on kind of guy. He may be caressing his infant son or slapping a cheeky magazine with an injunction. It's all part of a career—not to mention life—that has been micro-managed from Day One all the way to its current glorious incarnation as the most successful one in box-office history.

# EIGHTEEN

# Mission Possible

S herry Lansing had a problem. The current production chief at Paramount Studios, however, had always been good at problem-solving, but this time she was stumped. *The Firm*, starring Tom Cruise, had just made $158 million for her studio. (For the film's real gross, triple that figure to include video rentals and foreign, cable, and broadcast TV sales.) Lansing was desperate to hold on to Cruise's attention with another script he couldn't resist. The only problem for the executive was that none of the scripts she had lovingly proffered had interested him one bit.

Cruise had summarily turned down a Western, *Bitter Root*, to be directed by super-hot John McTiernan (*Die Hards 1 and 3*). Hoping to appeal to his love of skydiving, Lansing also suggested *Drop Zone*, an adventure comedy about parachuting daredevils.

No deal.

As if the challenge of finding a script Tom would even accept wasn't enough, Lansing also hoped to dispel her star's aversion to sequels. And she finally found a project that not only appealed to the picky superstar, but one that had sequel possibilities written all over it.

*Mission: Impossible*, the action series that aired on CBS from 1969 to 1973, focused on a group of highly specialized government agents, called IMF, who relied on split-second timing and sophisticated technology to pull off a caper each week in only sixty minutes. For the first few years of the series, the covert operation usually involved destabilizing some fictitious Eastern European country that was unfriendly to the United States. (This was, after all, the Nixon years.) Toward the end of its run, the *Mission: Impossible* team ran out of Euro-principalities and turned its attention to fighting organized crime in the US. (Someone joked at the time that if the ultracompetent IMF team had staged the Watergate break-in, Nixon would have served out his second term.)

*Mission: Impossible* was a favorite of Cruise's growing up. But even back then, the actor with a knack for script dissection felt there was something missing from the series. And it was something he would make sure the feature film version had plenty of—character.

"I enjoyed *Mission: Impossible* as a series, but even as a kid, watching the show, I thought, 'It's really about doing things. You never got into the characters.' I always thought it would be fun to make the movie showing what these characters were like."

So when Sherry Lansing came up with a feature film based on *Mission: Impossible*, Cruise loved the concept, hated the script. But he signed on anyway. And then the perfectionist who rewrote *Rainman* brought in a battalion of A-list writers to add character.

The original script had a dubious pedigree to begin with. It was written by the husband-wife team of Willard Huyck and Gloria Katz, whose claim to infamy are two-fold: They are the authors of *Howard the Duck* and the worst of the *Raiders* trilogy, *Indiana Jones and the Temple of Doom*. (That's the one its director, Steven Spielberg, felt compelled to publicly apologize to his fans for.)

When you're Tom Cruise, the number one box-office star of all time, you don't have to take potluck from the creators of *Howard the Duck*. A procession of classy writers went to bat on the (very) raw material that had originally piqued both Cruise's interest and distaste.

And what talent these rewrite men boasted—box-office success and Oscar-winning resumés. First tapped was David Koepp, the screenwriter of the huge blockbuster, *Jurassic Park*. Koepp was hardly a hack with a golden touch, however. He had also showed himself adept at writing compelling characters not in his two-dimensional dinosaur rampage, but in another film he wrote, *The Paper*, about a fictitious New York tabloid, which was filled with multidimensional journalists. (Conveniently forgotten, perhaps, by Cruise, were Koepp's turkeys, including *The Shadow* and the superstar superflop, *Death Becomes Her*, not to mention Rob Lowe's post-video big-screen outing, *Bad Influence*.)

*The Hollywood Reporter* breathlessly reported that it was Koepp's rewrite—for a cool million—that had nailed the script for Cruise. Maybe. But the script had already been touched by gifted hands before Koepp even got to do his rewriting.

It's testament to Cruise's clout that *before* Koepp took a swing at *Mission: Impossible*, Steve Zaillian was asked to contribute "extensive notes" for Koepp's utilization. Steve Zaillian is the other writer who made 1993 the best year of Steven Spielberg's life. While Koepp contributed *Jurassic Park* that summer, Zaillian turned out *Schindler's List* in the winter and won an Oscar the following spring for his efforts.

If Koepp was box-office royalty, Zaillian was the emperor of quality. But he was also a master of characterization—just what Cruise salivated over. Zaillian had also written *Awakenings*, a brilliant, character-driven piece starring Robert DeNiro as a catatonic mental patient and Robin Williams as the psychiatrist who briefly brings him out of his coma. Williams did the best, most modulated work of his career in that film, and DeNiro won his umpteenth Oscar nomination for it.

By now, Cruise's treasury of writers was looking like something out of Ali Baba's cave. The script, however, was still not good enough for the perfectionist superstar. Maybe he was so uptight about the quality of the material because the project represented his first outing as a producer. This film would have his name on it, not only "starring Tom Cruise" but as a "Tom Cruise presentation." (Paula Wagner, his former agent and current partner in his CW Productions company, would share the producer credit. An old hand, she was just more insurance that his maiden producing effort wouldn't crash and burn.)

According to the *Los Angeles Times*, which usually errs on the side of caution, not scandal-mongering, the oft rewritten script of *Mission: Impossible* was still showing its roots—TV.

The *Times* reported that Cruise loved the storyline, but hated the dialogue. One anonymous source was quoted as saying the script suffered from "bad dialogue and scenes that aren't being flushed out. In other words, a bad TV script."

To solve the problem, Cruise tapped a relatively new resource: the personal screenwriter. Just as every mover and shaker has his own personal trainer, nutritionist, astrologer, and shopper, superstars have a favorite screenwriter they call whenever they're in trouble.

Cruise's ace in the hole, Robert Towne, had worked with him on *Days of Thunder*. But Cruise fell in love with the screenwriter when he was called in to doctor the troubled script for *The Firm*. Towne reportedly cleaned up the plot's untidy denouement, and even more importantly for Cruise, fleshed out his arriviste character.

By the time Cruise flew to London in February to begin shooting his new film at Pinewood Studios, he still hated the script. As the *Los Angeles Times* said, "The script for the film of *Mission: Impossible* is turning out to be just that."

Again, demonstrating his amazing clout, the actor was able to summon Towne to London for one more rewrite.

Towne apparently did the trick. His rewrite of umpteen rewrites finally satisfied the superstar, and the director, Brian De Palma, was finally allowed to shout, "Action!"

The choice of De Palma was a curious one for Cruise as producer to make. De Palma has had more flops than hits, and his often ham-fisted direction has ruined many a brilliant script. (Remember the risible *Scarface*, written by Oscar-winner Oliver Stone?)

De Palma is also famous, or infamous, for piling up more dead bodies on film than the climax of *Hamlet*. Tom Cruise has said on the record that he hates violent films. He has only starred in one film that had lots of blood in it, *Interview with the Vampire*, which was literally a case of gore being integral to the plot and the characters.

But maybe Cruise was being savvy after all in approving the director. One of De Palma's few financial successes had been another TV remake, *The Untouchables*, although its rich characterizations no doubt owed more to the Pulitzer Prize-winning author of the script, David Mamet, than to the director.

De Palma may also have been a last minute replacement hired under the gun of a tight shooting schedule after Sydney Pollack, the director of *The Firm*, dropped out for unexplained reasons.

Cruise no doubt would have preferred the gilt-edged services of the director of *The Way We Were* and *Tootsie* over those of *Phantom of the Paradise*, but even his superstar clout, apparently, has its limits, and he was unable to hold on to Pollack. Pollack's refusal probably was caused by the quality of the script. Certainly it had nothing to do with his relationship with Cruise during *The Firm*. When that film came out, Pollack, who has worked with everyone from Robert Redford to Barbra Streisand, said that his experience with Cruise was one of the happiest of his career.

The film that was about to be shot in London looked like a sure bet, and at the same time it was something of a gamble.

Usually, Cruise leads the pack with his choice of film projects. During the cynical '80s, he reintroduced patriotism as a viable movie theme with *Top Gun*. This time with a TV remake, he was following a box-office trail already successfully blazed by Harrison Ford in *The Fugitive* and Mel Gibson in *Maverick*. *The Fugitive*, with its intense portrayal of Dr. Richard Kimble by Harrison Ford, was more character-driven and actually did twice as much business as the two-dimensional, jokey *Maverick*. Paramount executives were probably grateful for Cruise's costly rewrites of *Mission: Impossible* since they burnished the characters, and *The Fugitive*'s success showed that character paid off, even in action films.

While TV remakes had already proved themselves at the box office, Cruise took a gamble with the very nature of *Mission: Impossible*'s storyline.

It was an ensemble piece!

The most egoless of superstars, Cruise had chosen to star in a film where he was only one member of a group of starring actors. Maybe Cruise was wearing his producer's hat when he made the self-effacing decision to be just a member of the IMF team, although like Peter Graves in the TV series, he would surely be *primus inter pares*, first among equals.

However, Cruise wasn't so self-effacing when it came to the original cast of the TV series. The script has the audacious twist to invite Peter Graves, Barbara Bain, and Peter Lupus to reprise their original roles. Then in the first few minutes of the film, they all get mercilessly blown away—all except for the new member of the team, who happens to be Tom Cruise.

As the series used to say in its opening sequence, his task, should he choose to accept it, is to find out why the IMF team was killed and bring the culprits to justice. "As always, should you or any member of your IM force be caught or killed, the secretary will disavow any knowledge of your actions."

Besides being a plot point, another reason the original TV

cast gets dumped early on is that they are all has beens. Two of the original cast members who have gone on to greater fame, Leonard Nimoy as the director of two *Star Trek* features and Martin Landau who just won an Oscar earlier this year, did not deign to appear in the film for obvious reasons. No studio executive or scriptwriter would have had the temerity to off the respected Landau in the first five minutes of the film.

The new cast includes Emmanuelle Beart, Jon Voight, Jean Reno, Ving Rhames, and Henry Czerny, as well as Vanessa Redgrave as a villain named MAX. If none of those names besides Voight and Redgrave rings a bell, it's because A-list actors like Gene Hackman, who publicly proclaimed his satisfying experience with Cruise in *The Firm*, turned him down flat for the ensemble work in *Mission: Impossible*. Ditto John Malkovitch, who would have made a splendidly slimey villain. (Redgrave will do just fine, of course. In fact, the participation of the actress, whom *Time* magazine once called the greatest English-speaking actress of her age, in a pot-boiler like *Mission: Impossible* defies explanation.)

Voight plays a member of the IMF team as does Ving Rhames, the crime boss in *Pulp Fiction*. Henry Czerny, who played the duplicitous deputy CIA chief in *Clear and Present Danger*, gets promoted to the top post at the CIA in *Mission: Impossible*. Interestingly, the head of the CIA in this film is the bad guy, Cruise's chief nemesis in uncovering the fate of all those poor TV actors who get offed in the film's opening minutes.

The choice of Emmanuelle Beart as his leading lady is vintage Cruise. He adores exotic beauties, having personally chosen a relative unknown, Italy's Valeria Golino, to co-star in *Rainman*. Beart is gorgeous and a classy actress. She starred in the French classic, *Manon of the Spring*, opposite Gerard Depardieu.

She also looks a bit like the voluptuous first Mrs. Cruise, Mimi Rogers, which reminds us it was Rogers's absence from her husband's film *Days of Thunder* that allowed him to fall in love with his co-star, Nicole Kidman. Kidman wasn't taking any chances that history would repeat itself during the filming of *Mission: Impossible*. Not only did she fly non-stop from LA to London the very day she wrapped *Batman Forever*, she brought along their daughter and newly-adopted son as further ammunition to reinforce the family bond.

# NINETEEN

# King of Hearts

I t's a safe bet that Cruise will stay on top of his profession for the foreseeable future. His uncanny knack for picking the right projects at the right time suggests an almost psychic ability—or at least the eye of a pop sociologist who can spot trends, then dramatize them on screen.

"The most interesting thing about Cruise's career is its longevity, and he's only, what, thirty-one, thirty-two," says a journalist who's been covering the actor's career from its inception. "He's been a major box-office draw for more than a decade. His resumé is filled with one blockbuster after another. He's had a couple of misses, but mostly hits, $200-million hits."

It's virtually impossible to exaggerate the Olympian heights his career has reached. And that's not flackery. It's fact.

Just about every Tom, Dick, and Marilyn in the entertainment industry—past and present—has his or her star on the Hollywood Walk of Fame. But even the most famous stars have to pay the $1,500 fee to get his/her name imbedded in the pigeon droppings and cracked sidewalk cement. Some stars whose accomplishments entitle them to such immortalization have refused to pay and discouraged their movie studios, agents, and friends from forking out the dough. Meryl Streep and Paul Newman are among these star-less stars.

Often when a big movie comes out, the studio will foot the $1,500 bill to get the star of the film a sidewalk memorial. The wire services send a photographer, and the celebrity, kneeling down on the sidewalk as he lifts the cover off his star, gets his photo (and a mention of his new film) flashed around the world by UPI and AP. It's good, cheap publicity, and almost everyone who is anybody—and a lot of nobodies—has his or her star in the pavement.

Tom Cruise is no exception.

But there is something different and unique about his star; it's the only one that has to be regularly replaced. Vandals or film critics who hate his moviemaking aren't the culprits who destroy the star. Worshipping fans are. Cruise has gone beyond being merely an icon and become a secular saint. Fans chip away fragments of his sidewalk star to carry home. It's not unreasonable to say that his star on the Walk of Fame has become a relic of his sainthood, and devoted disciples want a piece of the true Cross—or ersatz Cruise.

In May of 1990, one fan went for the whole enchilada. According to the Hollywood Chamber of Commerce, someone took a hammer to the raised lettering that spells out the star's name and literally took home a piece of Tom Cruise.

This may sound like a typical chapter from the life of an overzealous fan, but it's not really typical at all. Laura Myer of the Hollywood Chamber of Commerce quipped, "It was the first time somebody did more than step on a star." And it was the first time a star had to be completely replaced. Not even Garbo or Elizabeth Taylor have engendered this kind of covetousness from fans. No one has tried to take home a piece of Elvis either, which is even more amazing. In the pecking order of celebrity saints, Tom Cruise is bigger than Elvis!

Cruise, the man with the Golden Gut, has shown an intuitive knack for capturing the *Zeitgest* of an era in his choice of projects. His filmography is a list of the nation's preoccupations and values at the time each film was made.

*Risky Business* was released just in time to miss the terror of AIDS and the new morality it ushered in. A sex farce about prostitutes, who would later be implicated along with intravenous drug users as the main vector of the disease into the heterosexual community, would have been unthinkable just a few years and 250,000 deaths from AIDS later.

*Top Gun* epitomized the jingoism and militarism of the Reagan-Bush years despite the efforts of its star to downplay that theme and emphasize male-bonding instead.

*Cocktail* tried to be a cautionary tale in the Decade of Greed, but no one picked up on its message while the economy continued to surge ahead.

The recession began in 1989, and Cruise once again had his finger to the wind and on the pulse of America.

*Born on the Fourth of July*, while dealing with issues twenty years in the past, reflected the general cynicism over governmental policy, whether government was lying about the Vietnam War or claiming good times were just around the corner.

*Far and Away* and *Days of Thunder* were pure escapism. Designed for a recession-weary public that stayed home and watched videos, which are a lot cheaper than going to the movies and paying $7.50 for a ticket and $5 for a box of stale popcorn.

*A Few Good Men* was 180 degrees away from the militaristic boosterism of *Top Gun* only six years in the past. With murderous Marines and an obstructionist commandant, the film explored the evil side of an organization that had been raised to the skies—literally—in the earlier film.

Both films reflected their particular place in time, and both cleaned up at the box office.

*The Firm* was an even bigger hit, and appealed to a public that had grown cynical about people in high places, from Michael Milken to Charles Keating.

He did it again with *Interview with a Vampire*, despite sharp criticism before the film was made and warnings that it would fail miserably. Cultish Rice fans insisted they would hate Cruise as Lestat, but he convinced them in the end that he was what they wanted after all.

As the recession recedes—even in California—Cruise once again has his eye on the bottom line.

Good times call for popcorn movies with no social conscience. *Mission: Impossible* is not exactly *The Grapes of Wrath* or even *Born on the Fourth of July* in terms of social-protest filmmaking.

And as sure as day follows night, Tom Cruise will eventually, probably sooner rather than later, put on the director's cap for a major project.

All the other superstars, with the exception of Dustin Hoffman, have itched to get behind the camera and put their vision on film.

Cruise has made the hallmark of his career stretching, challenging himself to try new things, whether it's playing a bisexual vampire or a paraplegic without bladder control.

Short of climbing Mount Everest with his bare hands, directing is the greatest challenge Cruise can take on at this point in his career.

He's already proved himself king of the hill at the box office. And he's shown himself to be a better TV director than many stars with his classy film noir effort on Showtime. All that's left is the step from TV to the silver screen.

The film project he chooses for his maiden effort behind the camera will say volumes about the star's character and aspirations.

Will he do a self-effacing "Robert Redford" and direct but not star as Redford did with *Ordinary People*? Or will he try a "Warren Beatty" and do a complicated but intellectually unchallenging popcorn film like *Dick Tracy*? Or will he give Kevin Costner a run for the Renaissance Man title, starring and directing a genuine epic like *Dances With Wolves*? Serious theme.

Complex characters. A technically difficult shoot. Even tricky animal stunts.

"When Tom finally tries his hand at directing," says an industry observer, "it will be the most organized project on any studio backlot. Everything will be perfect. He'll agonize over casting for months. Memos will fly back and forth between him and the suits in the executive suites. Then he'll cast his wife. Writers will tear their hair out as Cruise goes over and over the script until each role is perfectly tailored to each actor he's cast."

Whatever project Cruise chooses after *Mission: Impossible*, in front of or behind the camera, he will bring the same character traits and obsessions that date back to his formative years and that have given him one of the most successful film careers in the history of the dream factory.

# FILMOGRAPHY

**1981** *Endless Love*
Director: Franco Zeffirelli
Co-stars: Brooke Shields, Martin Hewitt

**1981** *Taps*
Director: Harold Becker
Co-stars: Sean Penn, Timothy Hutton, George C. Scott,
 Ronny Cox

**1983** *Losin' It*
Director: Curtis Hanson
Co-stars: Jackie Earle Haley, John Stockwell, Shelley Long

**1983** *The Outsiders*
Director: Francis Ford Coppola
Co-stars: Matt Dillon, Ralph Macchio, Patrick Swayze, Rob Lowe,
 Emilio Estevez, C. Thomas Howell

**1983** *Risky Business*
Director: Paul Brickman
Co-star: Rebecca De Mornay

**1983** *All the Right Moves*
Director: Michael Chapman
Co-stars: Paige Price, Christopher Penn, Lea Thompson

**1985** *Legend*
Director: Ridley Scott
Co-stars: Mia Sara, Tim Curry

### 1986  *Top Gun*
Director: Tony Scott
Co-stars: Kelly McGillis, Val Kilmer

### 1986  *The Color of Money*
Director: Martin Scorsese
Co-star: Paul Newman

### 1988  *Cocktail*
Director: Roger Donaldson
Co-stars: Brian Brown, Lisa Banes, Elizabeth Shue

### 1988  *Rainman*
Director: Barry Levinson
Co-stars: Dustin Hoffman, Valeria Golino

### 1989  *Born on the Fourth of July*
Director: Oliver Stone

### 1990  *Days of Thunder*
Director: Tony Scott
Co-stars: Robert Duvall, Randy Quaid, Nicole Kidman

### 1992  *Far and Away*
Director: Ron Howard
Co-star: Nicole Kidman

### 1992  *A Few Good Men*
Director: Rob Reiner
Co-stars: Jack Nicholson, Demi Moore

### 1993  *The Firm*
Director: Sydney Pollack
Co-stars: Gene Hackman, Jeanne Tripplehorn

**1994** *Interview with a Vampire*
Director: Neil Jordon
Co-star: Brad Pitt

**(In the works)** *Mission: Impossible*
Director: Brian De Palma
Co-stars: Emmanuelle Beart, Jon Voight, Jean Reno, Ving
       Rhames, Henry Czerny, Vanessa Redgrave